EPOXY RESIN ART FOR BEGINNERS

The New Step-By-Step Guide To Learning How To Make All Your Art Ideas Come True. Contains Easy Craft Projects With Color Images Of Jewelry, Tabletops, And Paintings.

Emma Woodhill

Table of Contents

INTRODUCTION

Art has always been a tool to communicate our feelings, desires, and abstract ideas that words cannot adequately describe. Painting and sculpture were once considered the pinnacle of artistic expression, and every other medium was seen as a novice's attempt to copy the greats. Today, we have no such pretenses, with installations and mixed-media artwork frequently combining elements that would never be seen together in another context.

Resin is a media that has suddenly gained popularity that seems to be only constrained by your imagination, but what is resin? What exactly can be made with it? Resin is becoming increasingly prevalent in crafting, so you might wonder what it is. And what exactly is epoxy resin? Epoxy resin is the substance, a two-part mixture of resin and hardener. When these two substances are combined, a chemical reaction takes place in which they chemically fuse to create a substance that resembles plastic.

After the now-fused resin has fully hardened, you're left with an incredibly adaptable, simple to use, resistant to extremes of heat and cold, and that can, if necessary, be drilled and sanded. For all kinds of applications, there are several kinds of resin, each with properties tailored to specific surfaces or for achieving a particular aesthetic. Some resin materials are even made to set and cure quicker, such as UV resin, which hardens and heals more quickly when exposed to UV light, either natural or artificial (also known as sunlight or UV lamps).

The resin is used in nearly every industry, including electronics, automotive manufacturing, insulating electrical wiring, and even construction tools, as a quick and efficient way to solve otherwise challenging engineering problems. It is also used to make lovely castings, paintings, and surfaces for furniture. Even though the resin is highly adaptable and simple to use in its two-part form, it can cause mild to moderate irritation if it gets in your eyes, on your skin, or if you unintentionally breathe in the fumes while it cures.

Even though working with any form of resin requires wearing gloves and a face mask, you should be aware that it's not always unsafe.

The resin is chemically inert once it has had time to cure fully. In reality, once the wax has fully hardened, it is safe for consumption. This means that the culinary industry can use resin in kitchen surfaces, fine cutlery, plate ware, and even containers for leftovers. Make sure you are using a resin graded for these applications, and always allow your next resin job to cure for the manufacturer's specified amount of time.

One of the most varied art forms available is resin, which may be used independently and complement other fields like installation art, painting, and furniture design. What precisely is resin art? For simplicity, I'll focus on the art that can create with resin. Resin art generally refers to anything produced for strictly aesthetic reasons by combining resin and hardener. This mixture is frequently laced into the mold of your choice, let to cure, and then the casting is removed, providing a good representation of the mold's inside.

is a high-quality method of recreating a shape, figurine, toy, jewelry, coaster, or any other potential ody. When the mood strikes, you might create ancient casts by covering the desired object in mold utty and letting it dry. The shape you've captured can then be replicated in resin form by pouring esin into the mold and adding color, items, glitter, and whatever else comes to mind.

he best thing about resin art is how versatile it is and how long-lasting it usually is. Resin art has the dded benefit of being personalized to you or anybody else you may want to give it to. Resin art lasts a lifetime and makes beautiful gifts for your friends and family.

his book introduces you to resin epoxy art for beginners through the instruction. Before starting, you ill discover what resin is and what to watch out for a while using epoxy resin. It will provide a step-by-step tutorial on making your first resin creation and show you where to buy the required materials. he following book contains all the essential information for a good start in casting resin.

CHAPTER 01
WHAT IS EPOXY RESIN?

Everything You Should Know About Epoxy Resin Art

Epoxy resin is a simple way to learn. You'll be astounded by the stunning artwork you can produce even as a beginner, and it's a beautiful way to explore your artistic side. The best aspect is that you always have new projects, methods, and ideas to try. Once you grasp the fundamentals of working with epoxy resin, you'll discover there are countless options!

Epoxy resin is unmatched in its adaptability and possesses an alluring beauty. It can create anything from 3-dimensional artworks and home décor to brilliant jewelry and unique furniture. Everything you'll need to start making resin art is in this introduction to epoxy resin.

When you get to the end of the chapter, you'll be well-equipped to answer any questions about epoxy resin art. Are you prepared to impress your friends—and perhaps even your clients—with some original epoxy resin creations? For inspiration, keep reading!

What Components Make of Epoxy Resin?

A transparent liquid plastic, epoxy resin, is composed of resin and hardeners. Let's examine the definition of "resin" first. Resin comes in two types: natural resin and synthetic resin.

What is natural resin?
Natural resin is a viscous liquid that plants exude for defense and therapeutic purposes. Natural resin's key characteristic is its ability to solidify and change into a translucent substance, utilized in various products like jewelry, fragrances, lacquers, and varnishes. Natural resin is costly because it is so hard to find.

What is Synthetic resin?
In the form of viscous liquids that solidify into a plastic surface, synthetic resin, also known as liquid plastic, is an artificial and more cost-effective alternative to natural resin. Epoxy resin, which is often comprised of polyester, silicone, or polyurethane, is the synthetic resin that is used the most widely. Because it is affordable, adaptable, and successfully mimics natural resins' liquid and solid qualities, epoxy resin is widely used.

Without a hardener, the synthetic resin cannot harden into a solid. Hardeners act as the resin's curing catalyst. They are epoxy's curing agents and are frequently made of amines and polyamides. The chemical reaction known as curing occurs when the synthetic resin is combined with an appropriate hardener.

At standard temperature, we are curing converts the two liquid substances into a complex, firm, and lustrous solid in a few hours. A high-gloss, crystal-clear surface is the result.

Resin art is a term used to describe art made with Epoxy Resin.

What is Epoxy Resin Art?

Epoxy resin is nearly universally mentioned when craftspeople and artists discuss the "resin" they use to make "resin art." Epoxy resin was initially employed in industrial settings. That is until photographers and painters realized that a glossy resin varnish gave works of art a sleek, contemporary finish and made the colors jump. Today's artists, designers, craftsmen, and DIY hobbyists are all completely obsessed with resin art, which has recently experienced a meteoric rise in popularity.

Many techniques can be employed with epoxy resin to produce artwork with outstanding depth and beauty. Here are a few of the most well-known works of resin art:

- Coasters & Trays
- Resin Castings
- Epoxy Countertops
- Abstract Art
- Flow Art Projects
- Jewelry Resin
- Resin Wood Lamps
- Sculptures
- Mosaics
- Resin Geode Art
- Resin Pens
- Charcuterie Platters / Serving Boards
- Flowers Preserved in Resin
- Epoxy Art Paintings
- Resin Tumblers
- Wood River Tables
- Resin Bar Tops

Epoxy resin can also be used as a topcoat to give drawings, paintings, and photographs a polished appearance while shielding them from harm and the damaging effects of UV light. The products produced by the addition of resin colorants and inclusions are intriguing. When dealing with epoxy resin, experimentation is essential whether you're a novice or an expert artist.

Is it Safe to use Epoxy Resin?

Different brands of epoxy resin have other qualities. To stretch the product, many brands use hazardous solvents and additives in their formulae. They have ominous warnings on the label and present the user with significant health hazards.

Fortunately, there is a brand that is non-toxic and has undergone the necessary testing to guarantee that your health and safety won't be jeopardized. For artists and crafters, ArtResin® Epoxy Resin was created. When used as instructed, this pure, low-odor product is secure for use at home. It doesn't make any fumes or volatile organic compounds (VOCs) that can irritate your lungs and doesn't contain any dangerous solvents.

Unfortunately, this is not the case for the majority of epoxy resin brands, so before you begin, always check the Safety Data Sheet for the resin brand you are using to make sure the product is safe or to make sure you are using the appropriate PPE, such as safety goggles and respiratory protection, to protect yourself.

Follow these common-sense safety precautions to avoid skin irritation, which can occur with any epoxy resin, regardless of brand:

- Use disposable nitrile gloves.
- Be sure to dress in long sleeves.
- Working in a room with open windows and doors will help you stay healthy.
- When working with resin, avoid food and drink.
- Keep away from children's and animals' reach.
- Never flush out any unused resin.
- Using a paper towel and isopropyl alcohol removes all resin stains from equipment, work surfaces, and clothing.

Which Resin Should I Purchase?

You may be tempted to purchase the cheapest epoxy resin when you begin working with resin. This is the kind of resin you want to avoid using! Inexpensive epoxy resins weren't made for artistic purposes. They frequently include harmful substances, release unpleasant smells, and turn yellow, damaging your artwork and costing you money. The adage "You get what you pay for" applies.

Ultimately, it's worth spending a little more to protect your health and artwork with a product like a premium, crystal-clear, non-toxic epoxy resin.

What Colors and Dyes Work Well With Resin Art?

Epoxy resin is colored using a wide variety of colorants by resin artisans. Each one has distinctive characteristics and outcomes that will influence the result. Among the most widely used resin colorants are:

- Mica powder
- Acrylic paint
- Powdered pigment
- Alcohol Ink, the specific colorant required for petri dish art
- Richly saturated ResinTint, explicitly designed for use with resin
- Glitter is not a true colorant but still provides a colorful effect

solid colors, metallics, neon/fluorescent effects, and pearlescent effects are just a few options for resin colorants. You have a choice!

Before adding your favorite epoxy colorant to color epoxy resin, combine the resin and hardener. Once the resin and pigment are appropriately blended, stir softly yet thoroughly.

The First Time Maker's Guide to Epoxy Resin Art

Have you thought about a project or a design you might start with, along with possible color schemes? Your first work of art made of epoxy resin is particularly remarkable, as we are well aware. We've developed a thorough 6-step tutorial that explains how to make resin art for the first time because of this.

1. Get your work area ready.

It's crucial to have a spotless, dust-free, and adequately ventilated environment when dealing with resin. To ensure that the resin cures uniformly, the surface you're working on needs to be completely level and protected with a plastic drop cloth. Can use a drop sheet to shield the floor from resin spills.

Before measuring and mixing, ensure that all the necessary instruments are available and that your piece is prepared and ready to go.

To ensure you have the necessary personal protective equipment for the resin you use, consult the Safety Data Sheet for the wax. Disposable gloves must be used when working with Art Resin, but other resin brands may call for respiratory protection or even safety goggles. Always read the SDS before you start, and be safe!

2. Measure the amount of epoxy resin you'll need.

To find the proper mixing ratio, refer to the instruction booklet. This is crucial because different resin brands may require different mixing ratios. When handling wet resin equipment or the resin bottles, and before you measure and mix, put on a pair of disposable nitrile gloves to protect your skin. Measure carefully because if you add too much resin or hardener, the chemical reaction will be changed, and the mixture won't cure properly.

3. Mix

While imagination and originality are crucial, patience is a quality from which epoxy resin artists and DIY producers benefit. Slowly combine the resin and hardener until they are thoroughly combined. Slow stirring is essential to prevent adding too many bubbles to the resin mixture.

Check the instruction handbook before mixing because mixing times can differ from brand to brand. For example, Art Resin epoxy requires a minimum of three minutes of mixing. As you stir, scrape the mixing bowl's sides and bottom. A reagent that has been mixed incorrectly and is left on the bottom and sides will not catalyze well, creating sticky stains that won't dry.

Even if you've mixed slowly, the resin mixture probably contains some bubbles. Don't worry; these bubbles will be dealt with after the resin is poured.

4. Beginner's Guide to Resin Pouring

The resin mixture should next be applied to your artwork. Before you pour, make sure your piece is dry and dust-free. The resin can be worked on for about 40 minutes before it gets too thick to run and distributed with a flat tool, such as a plastic spreader, to position the resin. Self-leveling art resin will begin to spread independently, but applying it will guarantee that the entire surface is equally coated.

Several options exist for how to handle the edges of your piece.

- Toto has the Art Resin sit domed on top of their piece; they should tape the sides and direct the resin to the edges. Remove the tape at the 24-hour mark to reveal the clean sides.
- Tape off the piece's bottom and let the resin drop over the sides before spreading it evenly with a foam brush or your gloved finger.

5. Finish Your Epoxy Resin Work

A quick pass of a flame torch can quickly eliminate air bubbles. Even though many tiny air bubbles may spontaneously pop, a clean, glass-like surface will result from an artist's torch pop.

Use a toothpick to remove any dust or hair that may have gotten stuck in the wet resin. B Defects can be seen by placing a light source on the spread-out resin.

The best tool for this is the flashlight on your smartphone. Your artwork should be protected with a box or tote made of plastic or cardboard. Ensure the lid is clean and within easy reach before you start to resin. If you do it this way, you won't have to leave your wet piece while looking for one.

6. Await Curing Of The Resin Artwork

Give the resin artwork at least 24 hours to cure in a place free of dust. The resin will become thick and tacky in 3 to 5 hours when you can pour a second coat.

The resin will be touch-dry and 95% cured in just 24 hours. You can hang your item on the wall or show it after 24 hours without worrying. Within 72 hours, it will be cured entirely, and you can ship it without risk.

Thank you for purchasing this book.

Scan the Qr Code to download your bonuses and leave a review.

We independent writers need your opinion, and by making this small gesture, you will give me a chance to be more visible than the big publishers.

Thank you so much for taking the time to do this.

CHAPTER 02
RESIN ART TOOLS FOR BEGINNERS

Using the proper tools for the job is a wise maxim when dealing with epoxy resin. To maximize your time, effort, and financial savings, it's critical to employ the appropriate equipment for the job at hand. Each resin tool has a unique function. You might not know where to begin, though, if you've never dealt with resin before:

- What equipment for resin art should a beginner buy?
- Which resin-related tools are necessary versus desirable?
- What stores sell resin tools?
- Do I have to spend much money on materials for art resin?

The good news is that simple resin art supplies are conveniently available online or at your local hardware store. They might even be lying about your house right now.

The prerequisites for using epoxy resin are as follows:

Supplies for Resin Art for Beginners

1. Epoxy Resin
2. Disposable Gloves
3. Butane Torch
4. Apron/Old Clothes
5. Plastic Drop Sheet
6. Masking Tape
7. Plastic Stands
8. Plastic Spreader
9. Toothpicks
10. Level
11. Plastic Measuring Cup
12. Plastic Stir Stick
13. Butane Torch
14. Dust Cover
15. Alcohol and Paper Towel
16. Butane Torch

The Value Of Plastic Resin-Based Tools

For a good reason, I advise using plastic equipment while working with resin, including stir sticks, spreaders, and plastic drop sheets. Who doesn't want rapid cleanup? Epoxy resin won't stick to plastic, making cleanup easy.

When it comes to degreasing equipment made of plastic resin, you have two options:

- Wet tools should be sprayed with isopropyl alcohol and dried with paper towels. To get rid of every last bit of resin, repeat this process as frequently as necessary. Tools should be properly dried before use after being washed in hot, soapy water until no more resin residue is visible.
- To allow the resin to solidify, leave wet tools on a plastic surface overnight. The following day, the resin will easily peel off.

In either case, plastic tools are a wise choice for dealing with resin because they can be used repeatedly.

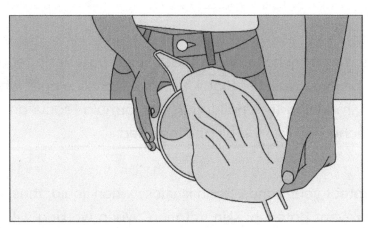

The Significance of Dry, Clean Resin Tools

It's critical to have the appropriate equipment for the work, but it's also essential that your resin tools are dry and clean:

- Dust, fragments of previously cured resin, solvents, or greasy substances can all contaminate resin from dirty instruments, preventing the resin from healing correctly.
- Water can result in a murky resin cure, so make sure your work area, measuring cups, tools, and the object you're resining are arid.

Essential Resin Art Tool Needs

A simple method to begin with epoxy resin and get a feel for it is to apply a coat on a piece of ar There are a few straightforward (but necessary) tools when working with epoxy resin. Let's look mor closely at the supplies you'll require to use epoxy resin as a surface coating:

1. Epoxy Resin

Depending on the scale of your project, epoxy resin materials are available in various volumes, fror 8 oz to 10 gallons. Uncertain of the quantity required? Resin Calculator (you can find it on Internet) w precisely calculate the amount of resin you need and which kit to purchase once you enter you dimensions.

A Remark on Respirators: You may have heard that using epoxy resin requires a respirator. This accurate for many resin brands available today. However, a toxicologist who examined resin foun that it is a clean system, meaning that nothing in the formula reacts and leaves any dangerou emissions that can be discharged into the air and ingested.

2. Gloves

Disposable gloves will protect your hands. Resin is sticky when liquid; thus, wearing gloves will kee your hands clean and prevent potential skin irritation. When working with resin, ensure you hav several pairs of gloves that prefer nerves since they resemble latex but are much more robust an don't include any of the allergic substances typically connected with latex. You may find nitrile glove in your accessory kit and the paint department of your local hardware shop.

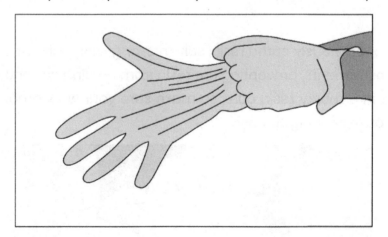

3. Old Clothes/Apron

Wear an apron, a smock, or old clothes while working to shield your clothing from resin drips. If you unintentionally spill any resin on your dress, there is no easy way to get it off. If you have long hair ponytail it to keep the resin out and the hair out of the resin.

4. Plastic drop sheet

Use a plastic drop cloth to prevent resin spills or drips on your work surface and floor. Paper towels and isopropyl alcohol can be used to clear resin drips, or if left too dry, they can be scraped off the next day. A clear, smooth vinyl shower curtain offers a cheap, durable liner that can be used repeatedly. Kitchen parchment paper is ideal for little jobs.

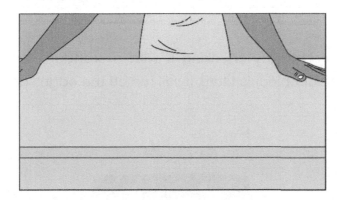

5. Masking Tape

Suppose you want to resin the piece's sides and tape off the bottom using premium painter's tape. This will prevent drips from ruining your artwork. Falls begin to build up around the base as resin drips down the sides due to gravity. The tape will catch these drips; you can remove the video and the beads together after the resin is touchably dry.

TIP: If you want to let the resin rest on top of your artwork or form a dome around it without spilling over the sides, you can tape off the bottom for extra stability.

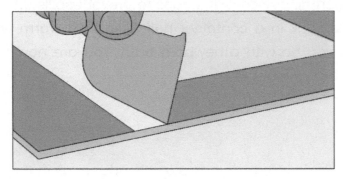

6. Stands

Extra resin can collect on the plastic-lined work surface when plastic stands to support your item. I use painter's pyramid supports; you can purchase them separately or as part of your Accessory Kit. You can get them in the paint area of any hardware store. Large plastic shot glasses or toy building blocks also work nicely; both can be found at the dollar store.

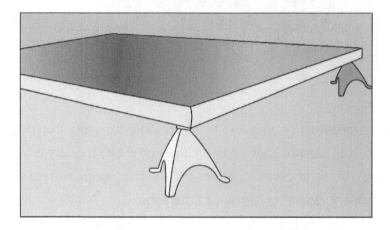

7. Level

Make sure your work is horizontal by checking it with a standard level. Due to the self-leveling properties of epoxy resin, if your object is tilted, it will run off the edges at the lowest point.

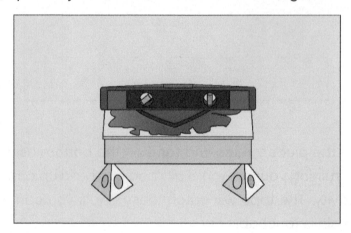

8. Plastic Container For Water Bath

If your resin is excellent, a warm water bath will bring it to room temperature and make it easier to handle. Choose a narrow container with high edges to prevent spills and keep the bottles uprights. The capped bottles should soak in a container half-filled with warm water for 10 to 15 minutes, approximately as long as you do with a newborn bath. You are now prepared to measure and combine after properly drying your bottles.

9. Stir Stick

The most excellent stirring device for resin has a level surface; resin that isn't well combined won't cure properly, so be sure to scrape the container's edges and bottom as you st ensure that all of the resin and hardener are blended. The container can be squeezed much more successfully and stick with a flat surface than t can with a round object, like a spoon. Tongue depressors made of wood can be used, but they must be thrown away after each usage.

10. Mixing Container

Use a plastic, graduated measuring jug to correctly measure and mix your resin because poorly measured resin and hardener won't cure. This makes it crucial to use a cup with clearly delineated lines to prevent guesstimating. As long as all the components weigh the same, it doesn't matter whether you consider weigh the resin or the hardener. Pick a plastic mixing cup, and when you're done, flip it over onto a surface covered in plastic to allow the resin to collect. Once the resin has dried the following day, you can peel it off and reuse your cup.

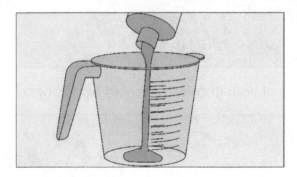

11. Spreader

Pinning epoxy resin will naturally self-level, but a flat plastic spreader evenly distributes it over your work. To direct the resin, use a plastic spreader with a flat edge.

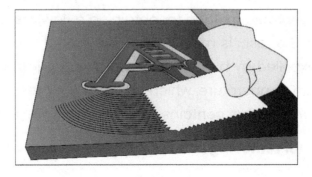

If you want to cover a particular species of your object, you can apply epoxy Resin there using a toothpick, a popsicle stick, or an old paintbrush.

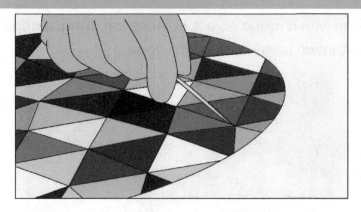

If you want the resin to sit perfectly in a dome on top of your artwork without spilling over the sides, small spatula or a plastic takeout knife works amazingly to push it up to the edge without spillin over.

You can apply resin to the sides of your item with gloved hands or a foam brush.

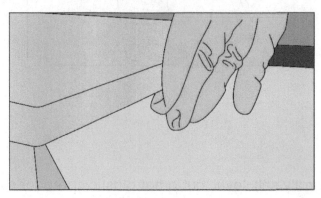

12. Torch

A flame torch is the most acceptable method for obtaining a flawless, bubble-free finish. Numerou bubbles are produced when the resin is mixed; if not eliminated, these bubbles will cure into you sculpture. They cannot be expelled by blowing into a drawing pricked with a toothpick. Hairdryer don't heat up to a hot enough temperature, which will blow your resin around and add dust. Whe working with silicone molds or resin that contains alcohol ink, a heat gun is a suitable option.

Nothing beats a flame torch for removing bubbles from most resin work.

A small butane torch, works well for most applications, except for liquid alcohol ink dropped into liquid resin, which is combustible. A propane torch is tough to beat for larger objects! Any hardware store will have tanks for butane and propane.

TIP: Please don't be anxious about using a flame torch. You'll wonder how you got along without one after using one.

13. Toothpicks

When resining, toothpicks are a necessity. After torching your item, hold it to the light at eye level to check for stray bubbles and fish out any hair or dust particles. They come in handy if you need to move tiny bits of resin or precisely position inclusions like jewels or gold flakes.

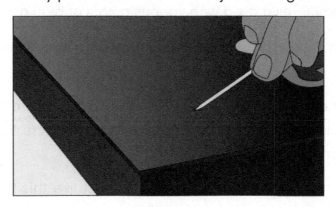

14. Dust Cover

Before beginning to resin, prepare a dust cover since you never want to expose your newly resined artwork while searching for a cardboard box or plastic tote. Wipe the cover surface to prevent dust from getting into your wet item. Since plastic totes are easy to clean, I prefer using them. Make careful to remove the flaps from the cardboard box you use. You don't want When you awaken the following morning, you don't want to find that a flap has fallen and cemented into your resin

15. Paper towel and alcohol

For spills and cleanup, paper towels and isopropyl alcohol are needed. Wearing gloves, remove as much wet resin as you can with paper towels before misting your equipment with alcohol to eliminate any remaining residue.

Repeat this procedure until there is no residue, then wipe dry with an extra paper towel. Resin should never be flushed down the toilet! After removing all resin residue from your instruments, wash them in hot, soapy water and allow them to dry thoroughly before reusing them.

TIP: Since alcohol destroys resin, you should avoid using it to remove resin from your hands because your skin can absorb it.

16. Hand Cleaner

Use an exfoliating hand cleaner to get rid of sticky hands. If Resin unintentionally gets on your skin, wash it off right once to prevent potential skin sensitivity. The hand cleanser with an exfoliation from the hardware shop is excellent. In a hurry, dry rubbing your hands to remove resin can be accomplished using a few poppy seeds and liquid soap. Give your hands a thorough water rinse after that.

Nice haves: Trying out resin

Here, you are free to showcase your talent! When you have a firm grasp of the principles, you'll be ready to experiment with new resin projects. Here are several places for novices to start:

- Create coasters and other small castings using silicone molds.
- Pour resin into alcohol ink to create petri dish art.
- Pouring several tints of colored resin results in flow art.
- To make ocean art, layer resin dyed with various colors of blue and white.

You'll need to upgrade your resin toolbox with the following items to complete these projects:

1. Silicone Molds

Unlike rigid plastic molds that could shred or deform, silicone molds are flexible and straightforward ove from the resin cast, making them perfect for little resin art projects. You can use them again and time again because it returns to their original shape.

Molds are available ly every size and form, but using a cast like this to produce resin coasters is straightforward. Beer caps, shells, vibrant stones, diamonds, crystals, and other inclusions are all possible.

A 2-part silicone substance called Mold Making Material enables you to make custom molds.

2. Alcohol Ink

You can also make petri dish resin art using a silicone mold. Pour a few drops of Alcohol Ink into some epoxy resin and put it in a silicone mold to produce tendrils, squiggles, and other fantastic effects. The colors are then forced down through the resin by a white ink sinker!

Please Be Aware: Alcohol ink is flammable, so avoid using a torch when working with it. While the liquid resin is not flammable, adding alcohol ink changes this. Most resin bubbles will usually pop due to the alcohol in ink, but if you need an extra boost, use a heat gun.

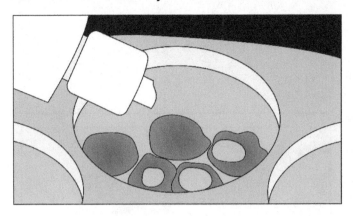

3. Colorants

When colored, epoxy resin has a lovely appearance; for optimal effects, always use a colorant made especially for resin, such as ResinTint liquid colorant. Once the resin has reached a single, uniform int, stir in the colorant.

TIP: No matter the kind, colorants shouldn't be used on more than 6% of the resin and hardener mixture's volume. If you do, your resin might not cure properly.

4. Stirrers and Plastic Cups

If your resin art project calls for colored resin, Mix it as follows using popsicle sticks and transparent plastic drinking glasses:

- You should combine all the resin you'll need for your project in one sizable batch.
- Depending on how much resin you need for each color, portion it into separate cups. For each hue, use a different cup.
- Add the tint to the resin and thoroughly mix it to get a uniform hue. If you start with less color than you think you'll need, you can always add more later.
- You can check the color's intensity by pulling a small quantity of tinted resin up the side of the plastic cup; if more tint is needed, add it immediately.

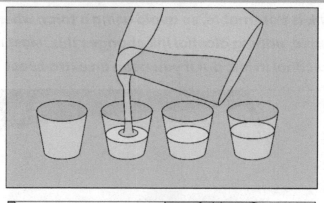

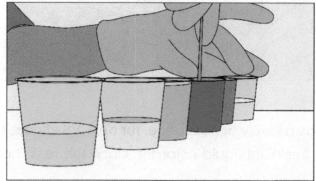

5. Metal Trays & Wood Panels

Epoxy resin weighs a lot. Therefore, when working with resin, wood panels are the best option. The most excellent substrates for holding resin weight are solid ones. Mount prints, images, or even pair directly onto the panel and cover with resin for a modern style. Cradled panels are an excellent optio for pouring colorful resin into ocean art since they have a lip to keep the resin. For this use, meta serving trays are also ideal

TIP: To prevent the stretched canvas from sagging and causing the resin to cure in a pool in the middle, the back must be reinforced with cardboard before resigning.

6. Heat Gun & Hair Dryer

Though I usually advise using a flame torch, there are three exceptions: Use a hair drier and a hea gun to create flow art on silicone molds.

- **When using alcohol ink:** A flame torch can cause a fire since alcohol is combustible. If yo need an extra boost, please use a heat gun. The alcohol in ink usually pops many resin bubble on its own.

- **When utilizing silicone molds:** A heat pistol is a good substitute when dealing with mold because a flame's intensity runs the risk of harming silicone.

- **For making cells and incorporating them into flow or ocean art:** Push the colored resin layer lightly with a heat tool or hair dryer set to low to produce entertaining results. Finally, swiftl eliminate any bubbles from the surface by fast passing a flame torch over it.

7. Inclusions

Include gold leaf, crystals, decorative stones, charms, glitter, and other fun small embellishments in your work to add shine, intrigue, and texture. "inclusions" refers to all the charming small accents you may incorporate into your resin product. Gold leaf flakes can be suspended, crushed glass or crystals can be added to imitate geodes, glitter can be used to create depth and brightness, and dried flowers, shells, or bottle caps can be used to construct coasters.

There are a million items you can add to the resin at the craft store; always ensure your inclusions are completely dried, and I recommend testing first to ensure you get the desired outcome.

1. SandPaper

You might occasionally discover that your resin has hardened but still contains a bubble, some dust, or even hair. Don't worry; this may be quickly repaired by applying a new resin coat. To prepare the initial coat so that the new resin has something to stick to, you must sand it down first. Using a piece of sandpaper, a sanding block, or an electric sander, sand the entire surface with coarse sandpaper, such as 80 grit. Pay special attention to sanding out the trouble spot. It will appear to be a mess, but don't be concerned. It will seem new once you remove the sanding dust and apply your fresh coat.

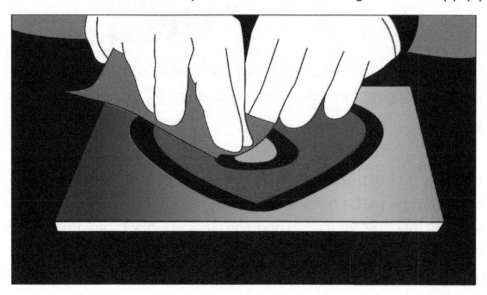

I sincerely hope this was useful. The bottom line is that having the proper instruments while working with resin assists you in producing better results.

CHAPTER 03
TOP 8 EASY RESIN ART PROJECT IDEAS FOR BEGINNERS
5 TIPS TO AVOID BUBBLES IN EPOXY RESIN

8 Easy Resin Art Project Ideas For Beginners

Do you want to attempt to create some resin art for yourself? Epoxy resin has many creative uses, such as coating artwork, pouring coasters, flow art, trinket dishes, and more! Here is a list of ten original resin art concepts suitable for novice and seasoned artists. Which one are you most eager to try?

1. Petri Dish Art

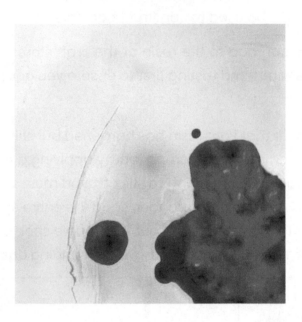

Alcohol ink is mixed with resin to create Petri Dish Art, cast in a reusable silicone mold. As the ink penetrates the polish, bright ribbons and multicolored "petrified" squiggles are produced.

How to Make A Resin Petri Dish

Before starting:

- Before combining, reheat the resin and hardener bottles in a warm water bath. Any bubbles that later try to escape will be helped.
- Put on gloves and measure your resin and hardener equally by volume while working in a well-ventilated location.
- For at least three minutes, thoroughly combine the ingredients while scraping the sides and bottom of the basin.
- Each mold component should contain half of the resin.

You're now prepared for the enjoyable part!

Step 1:

- 5-10 drops of Ink Sinker should be added to the Resin.

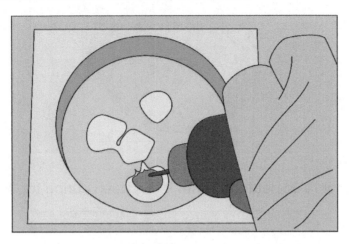

Step 2:

Add 5-10 drops of pink or red alcohol ink to the white.

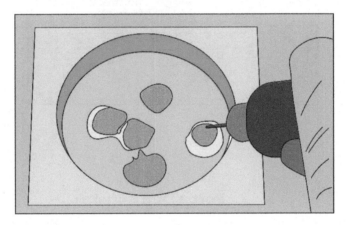

Step 3:

Apply 10-20 drops of gold alcohol ink on top of the pink/white drips you applied in Steps 1 and 2 and over the remaining resin surface.

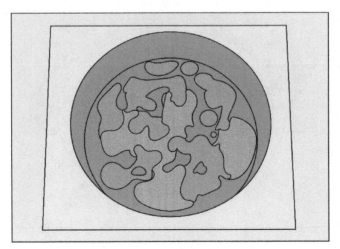

Step 4:

• Add five drops of whitening, 10–15 drops of pink OR red, then pink or red.

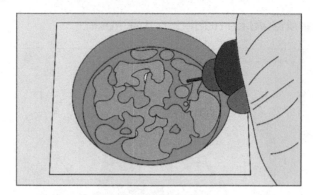

Peel the silicone mold of your resin petri dish after it has been curing for 24 hours.

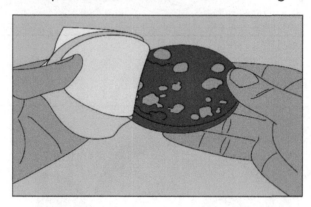

And It's Ready

2. Bottle Cap Coaster

Why not put your beer on a cap rather than a cap on your beer? While there are many other styles and hues of coasters, a resin coaster filled with your favorite beer caps will surely attract everyone's attention. Use your preferred soft drink caps if beer is not your thing.

3. Flow Art Tray

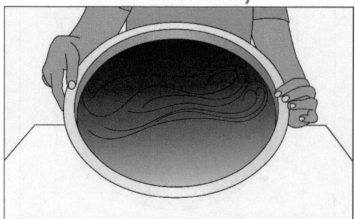

Flow with it!

Add some colored Resin on a cheap serving tray to make it seem better! They are helpful and lovely and make for interesting discussion pieces.

How To Create A Resin Flow Art Tray:

1. **Before you begin, assemble your materials:**

Before you begin, gather your tools and make sure your dust cover is nearby.

When creating your design and selecting your color scheme, keep in mind the color of your background. For instance, if your location is white, you can get away with translucent colors, whereas a dark or metallic background will benefit from opaque colors.

2. **Get Your Resin And Tints Ready:**

The resin and hardener should be mixed well for at least three minutes while scraping the bottom and sides of the mixing container in equal parts. Give each color its miniature plastic cup, then sprinkle the resin equally.

Each cup of resin should be tinted with a few drops of ResinTint, which should be added in small amounts and thoroughly mixed. Don't be scared to mix and combine different colors to get the colors you want.

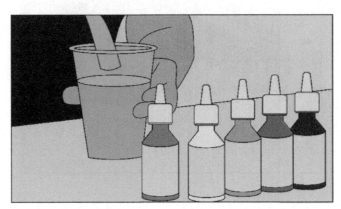

3. **Pour The Resin**

The enjoyable part now! Pour the darkest color first—in this example, navy blue—on the tray's side

closest to you.

Pour the white over the opposing side next.

If desired, you can overlay the two whites to add depth and a marbled appearance by varying the opacity of the white. Use a spreader or tilt the tray to reposition the tint and alter its shape.

In addition to the blue, add a turquoise ribbon by applying some to the tray and some over the dark blue. Finally, add gold to the vacant spot. To ensure no bare places, tilt the tray or use the spreader.

The Artist's Torch can be used to blow bubbles away. Before blending, let the resin sit for around 15 minutes. This will slow the movement and maintain the integrity of your pattern by allowing cells to grow and the polish to thicken.

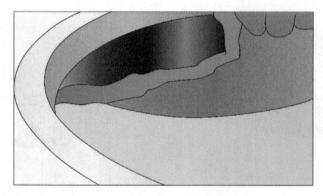

4. Create Your Design:

Before beginning to build your pattern, ensure the resin has had 15 minutes to settle and thicken. The resin is too fluid to blend straight away; you'll get muddy colors and lose your design. To make a pattern in the wax, carefully and organically combine the colors with a spatula.

When pulling the colors out so they can combine, use gradual movements but don't be afraid to go a little deeper. The shape you design will be preserved because the resin has thickened.

5. Torch, Cover, And Wait:

To eliminate any last bubbles, lightly run the torch over your artwork. When your item is dry to the touch, cover it with a dust cover and cure it for 24 hours.

Now It's Ready.

4. Puzzle

Puzzles are enjoyable, beautiful, and require no disassembly. After you've finished the last satisfying piece, choose a puzzle you'd love to display on your wall and cover it in resin to preserve it so you may keep enjoying it.

How To Resin A Puzzle

1. Choose a puzzle

Select a game that you like. Find a high-quality puzzle with sturdy pieces that fit tightly and have the image firmly attached without lifting, even though numerous variations are available. These problems could cause the resin or sealer to leak into your puzzle pieces, causing dark stains to appear along the seams. Poorer puzzles contain thin, usually misshapen parts that don't fit together and occasionally even have graphics peeling away at the edges.

2. Assemble your Puzzle

Put your puzzle together and use your preferred brush-on sealer to seal it. I suggest using a brush-on glue like ModPodge rather than a spray sealer since it will allow you to get in between the puzzle

pieces and prevent the resin from seeping in. Use a gloved hand, a brush, a foam brush, a plast
spreader, or another tool, as I did. Be sure to cover the outside edges of the problem as well.

Allow the sealant to finish drying.

***TIP: If the conundrum is of lower quality, you may want to apply 2-3 coats to ensure the problem
is thoroughly sealed. Between coats, the sealant must be entirely dry.***

3. Place a Thin Coat on

Apply a tiny layer of ModPodge or glue to the back of your sealed puzzle while flipping it over, ensurin
it covers the entire surface.

4. Mount the Puzzle

Place the puzzle on the board. To ensure the puzzle adheres to the board, brayer the entire surfac
and then place a piece of paper on top to protect it. We are focusing primarily on the borders. Giv
the adhesive time to dry completely.

5. Use plastic stands to support your artwork.

Use plastic stands to support your item once the adhesive has dried (I used turned-over plasti
cups.) Now that you are ready to begin!

6. Determine how much resin is required.

Use Resin Calculator to enter the length and breadth of your project to determine how much Resi
you'll need. For a typical 1/8" coating, a 12 by 12" piece of artwork requires 5 oz of resin (2.5 oz resi
and 2.5 oz hardener).

7. Stir Thoroughly.

Wearing gloves, measure out precisely equal amounts of resin and hardener. While stirring for
minutes, carefully scrape the sides and bottom of the mixing bowl.

8. Pour the Resin

Pour the resin into the middle of your piece and spread it to the edges using a plastic spreader or
popsicle stick. Before the resin becomes too thick, you'll have around 45 minutes to work with it.

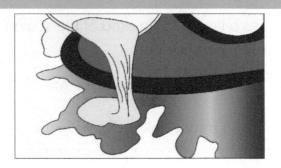

9. Put your artist's torch to use.

Just long enough to cause the bubbles in the resin to pop, hold the flame of your Artist's Torch a few inches above the resin surface while continuously moving the torch from side to side.

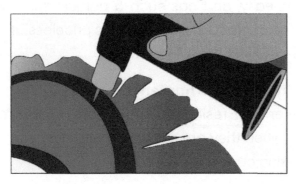

10. Check your work

Using a toothpick, search the resin in the light after the item has been torched for any missed bubbles, hairs, or dust particles.

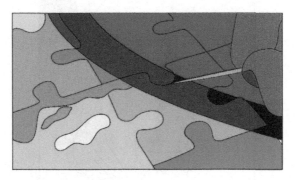

11. Wait 24 hours while you cover your puzzle.

For 24 hours or until it feels dry, cover your piece with a plastic bag or a cardboard box (with the flaps removed).

After 24 hours, make your content public!

TIP: The resin should feel dry to the touch after 24 hours. Your artwork is yours to hang and enjoy, but if you want to pack it up and move it, you must wait at least 72 hours for the resin to be correctly set.

5. Add A Resin Accent

Add a Resin "accent" to a work of art that is already created or one of a kind.

To add some more oomph, choose a tiny or large area of the sculpture and decorate it with resin. It lends depth to a flat piece and is shiny and smooth.

6. Upgrade Your Art

A little paint or a glossy layer of resin may transform a work of art! When you find an item that is *almost* perfect but needs a little something extra, it's a fantastic alternative.

7. Trinket Dish

Where do you put your change? Maybe your earring? Possibly paper clips?

Making your trinket dish is fun, easy, and has such a unique appearance that you'll find yourself placing them all over your home or place of business. It is priceless art!

How To Create Trinket Dish Art

1. **Pour warm water over the resin and hardener.**

Start by soaking your hardener and resin bottles in warm water for approximately 10 minutes. Removing them from the bath when they are still warm will allow you to measure equal amounts of resin and hardener for your mixing cup.

For each trinket dish mold, you will need roughly 2 oz—1 oz of resin and 1 oz of hardener. For at least three minutes, whisk the mixture gently. To prevent creating many bubbles, try to stir slowly.

2. **Put your silicone mold into the cardboard container.**

Repackage your silicone mold in the kit's cardboard box so that it can collect any spillage. Pour the mixture into your silicone mold once the resin and hardener have been properly blended. Each mold should be filled.

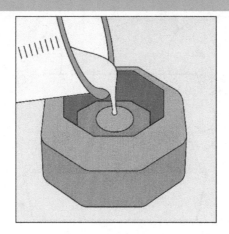

3. Use the alcohol ink

Now is the enjoyable part! Drop your chosen colors straight into the resin from the alcohol ink bottle. After using the stain, place a white Alcohol Ink Sinker over each color drop. Continually alternate between color and ink sinker until you're happy with the design!

Tip: When blending paint, use about two drops of color to one depth of ink sinker. This facilitates adequate stain penetration into the resin. For the resin to catalyze correctly, you need only 75–100 drops for each mold.

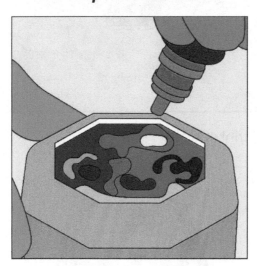

4. Close the cardboard kit box

Complete at this time! Cover the mold with the cardboard kit box after adding the ink, and allow it to set overnight (between 12 – 24 hours).

The following day (or after around 10 to 12 hours), you can remove your cured trinket dish from the silicone mold to see how it turned out.

Prepare yourself for a stunning color surprise!

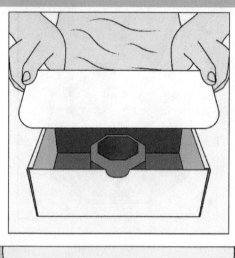

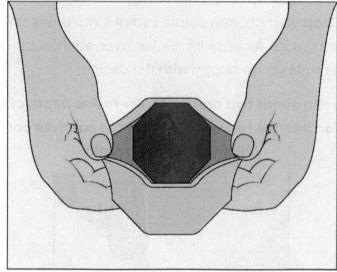

You've just made your functional trinket dish!

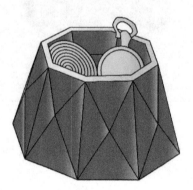

8. Jewelry Pendants

Sometimes all you need to level up your outfit is something easy and trim to make. Jewelry pendants are the ideal approach to display your originality and artistic flare to the world.

5 Tips To Prevent Bubbles In Epoxy Resin

Bubbles might be one of the most significant obstacles when using epoxy resin.

There are four primary causes of bubbles in resin that you could encounter:

- Not adhering to recommended epoxy resin processes
- Cold conditions
- Too thick of a pour
- There may be trapped air released by the artwork (this is often the case with paper and organic materials like wood, leaves, dried flowers, etc.)

When using resin, follow the following guidelines to help prevent air bubbles:

- **Use a Torch:** A torch is the best instrument for removing bubbles. The flame instantly heats the resin surface, thins it out, and causes bubbles to release.
- **Work in a Warm Environment:** For a resin with a crystal clear look and honey-like consistency that flows and spreads quickly, Ensure that your workspace is a little warmer than ambient temperature (75-85F or 24-30C). Epoxy resin enjoys being warm. When the resin is thick, murky, and appears milky due to hundreds of tiny bubbles that you won't be able to burn out, the temperature is too low.
- **Pour in layers of 1/8":** If the resin is poured thicker than 1/8" because bubbles won't escape to the surface, the resin will cure.
  Tip: The resin will cure if it is poured thicker than 1/8" because bubbles won't be able to rise to the surface.

How Easy Is Resin Art?

Epoxy resin art may seem scary at first. Still, if you try it, you'll understand why it's such a rewarding, imaginative activity for creative types like artists, crafters, and DIY enthusiasts. Once you master it, you'll be motivated to take on more challenging tasks and experiment with novel ways.

CHAPTER 04
HOW TO CHOOSE RIGHT EPOXY RESIN FOR YOUR APPLICATIONS
THE COMPLETE INFORMATION SOURCE FOR RESIN

Epoxy resin is more resistant to heat, chemicals, and mechanical stresses than other resin forms and has a wide range of industrial applications. Epoxy resin is applied in layers over a substance or poured into a mold when liquid to provide a protective outer covering. The meaning becomes solid, durable, and structurally sound after curing.

Epoxy resin is very helpful in various applications, from industrial tools to creative endeavors and the production of automobiles, thanks to this mix of properties. The fundamental properties of an epoxy resin formula will vary depending on the precise chemistry and polymerization techniques used.

What is Epoxy Resin?

Epoxy resin is a form of artificial resin that has several applications. Epoxy is created by combining two complementary components. A chemical reaction usually lasts many hours when the liquid resin is mixed with the proper hardener.

After the components are joined, the material changes from a liquid to a solid and produces heat. For the material to fully cure, the resin to hardener ratio should be either 1 to 1 or 1 to 2.

According to the manufacturer's instructions, several synthetic or epoxy resins can be employed for various applications and have varying qualities. Different kinds of resins significantly affect how long they take to cure, how hard they are, and how sensitive the finished surfaces are.

Heat resistance and the maximum layer thickness that can be applied to the substance are other factors to consider when selecting the best epoxy resin.

Epoxy resin's various qualities in various product varieties:

- Viscosity (flowability)
- Heat-resistance
- Electrical insulation
- Anti-corrosive
- Chemical stability
- Low moisture absorption
- Durable adhesive bond
- Low shrinkage after curing
- Absence of VOCs (volatile organic compounds)
- Excellent fatigue strength and flexural strength

What is the Purpose of Synthetic or Epoxy resin?

Epoxy resin, in general, is adaptable and can be used for various art and craft applications. The following things are possible uses for epoxy resin:

- Acrylic bar tops
- Soil Sealing in residential areas
- Resin-based Wood Stabilization
- Model construction projects
- Production of resin jewelry
- Shower tray shelves made of resin
- Kiteboards can be built on your own.
- Quick fixes using a specific UV resin
- Indoor and outdoor stone carpet repairs
- Waterproof epoxy coatings for garage floors
- Putting small parts together and repairing the
- Constructing one's terrariums and aquariums.
- Epoxy resin artworks, including resin art paintings
- Epoxy mold casting and many types of figurines
- Kitchen resin countertops sealed to prevent cutting
- Ideas for modern rehabilitation of historic structures
- Items for decoration like resin geodes and Petri dishes
- Synthetic resin can be used to cast objects and artifacts.
- Useful items made of wood with epoxy resin, such as cutting boards
- Furniture that endures, like river tables constructed of epoxy resin
- Artificial resin used as a topcoat or Gelcoat while manufacturing boats

What to Look out For When Purchasing Epoxy Resin?

Epoxy resin is available from several specialized dealers and most home improvement stores. The selection is considerably more extensive, and the supplies are frequently less expensive if you order online. Numerous internet retailers likely provide the broadest assortment of high-quality items .for all conceivable purposes.

The relatively high cost of many synthetic resin components may deter you if you begin working with synthetic resins. But it would help if you didn't look for the cheapest deals. Very inexpensive goods may be of worse quality, which might be visible in the outcome of your labor and demoralize you.

Some products might also include solvents that are unhealthy for the body or that evaporate during the curing process. This may cause the substance to cure or make it challenging to combine partially. Additionally, some less expensive epoxies process somewhat brownish rather than being transparent and crystal clear. A little sunlight can subsequently amplify this yellowish tint.

Tip: To make sure that your job is practical and that your results are satisfying, you should buy the best resin components you can afford even after completing a careful pricing comparison.

Which Epoxy Resin is Best For Your Project?

The ideal epoxy resin for your project will be determined by the material qualities that define a particular epoxy resin combination. You should be able to infer how the resin can function in its liquid and cured phases based on the manufacturer's specifications.

Casting resins / Low Viscosity Epoxy Resins

Viscosity describes a liquid's capacity to flow. But take note: A liquid is said to have low viscosity if it is delicate and freely flowing. If you want a low-viscosity casting resin, choose an epoxy resin. For a variety of uses, like the casting of molds or the construction of river tables, an almost watery consistency can be essential.

The cure for these extremely low and low viscoelastic epoxy resins is relatively slow. There should be more time between the future processing steps on your calendar. However, you also have a lot more processing time and less stress as a result. The typical curing time for low-viscosity synthetic glue is between 12 and 24 hours. Since the exothermic chemical transformation process is so slow, relatively little heat is generated. As a result, compared to epoxy resins with high or medium viscosities, thicker layers and larger quantities of the resin can be processed fast in one step.

Applications for casting resin include:

- Casting of several mold types
- Jewelry made of epoxy resin is made
- Molding of parts for the model-making industry
- Furniture creation, including resin river tables and epoxy resin tables
- Epoxy for wood crack and hole filling
- Production of epoxy resin for use in garage or living space floors

Epoxy resins (highly viscous), laminate resins, and countertop resins

Honey's stiff texture is reminiscent of extremely or moderately viscous synthetic resins, which are much denser. The many items in this category are frequently referred to as resin or laminating resin in the trade. They function best when applied to coated surfaces.

They can also be utilized to carry out undertakings in the areas of resin geodes and resin art. When using highly viscous epoxies, you must adhere to the manufacturer's recommended maximum layer thickness for each step. A maximum layer thickness on topo centimeters for trouble-free processing is frequently needed.

Laminating resin used for the following purposes:

- Epoxy resin is used to cast paintings as resin art.
- Petri dishes made of resin and resin Geoden are decorative pieces.

- The completion of all kinds of paintings and art pieces.
- A few types of jewelry made from epoxy resin.
- Surface sealing for tables or worktops.

Overview of the Various Viscosities

Layer Thickness

Due to the resin's lower thermal conductivity during curing, thicker layers can easily be cast using low-viscosity epoxy resins. You can gently remove air bubbles from the epoxy resin layer using a hairdryer or a Bunsen burner that is suitable for the task, if it does include any.

However, you shouldn't pour more than one centimeter thick (such as laminating resin). Due to its thick viscosity, it is challenging to induce air bubbles to rise and escape from the resin.

TIP: The most crucial details are often listed under the manufacturer's information on a product's box. Most of these items also reveal how much material is usually a single process.

Processing Time

When working with epoxy resins, the processing time—also referred to as the pot life or open time—is essential. The period before processing epoxy resin combined with a hardener is specified. The resin thickens and toughens after a certain point and shouldn't be used any longer (except in exceptional cases). After t that, it can no longer be colored consistently and cannot level out into a flat surface.

Short Processing time

Pros:
- Distinct epoxy compositions can provide different impacts while a person is dying.
- Quick layer buildup because more layers can be placed on top of one another more often.

Cons:
- More bubbles are produced as the venting scenario becomes more complex.
- When exposed to UV light, yellow coloration is possible.

Long Processing Time

Pros:
- You can combine various colors and complete your work in silence.
- The transitions between the layers are hardly noticeable when several transparent layers are stacked on top.

Cons:
- More unusual materials are required to cast numerous layers (mixing cup, spatula).

Curing Time

In the case of synthetic resin, the curing time is the period after the components have been mixed before a condition of complete totals and insensitivity has been attained.

most circumstances, processing time and curing time are correlated: If processing time is constrained, the resin usually cures completely, even quickly.

What degree of variation exists between the processing times for the various products?
The curing phase for items lasts about 24 hours, while processing takes 20 to 1 hour on average, with processing times of up to 12 hours and a complete cure time of up to one with whether the rein can be processed and used for more complex effects.

Properties of epoxy resin at a Glance

Synthetic resin production and sales have significantly increased in recent years. This astounding growth can be attributed partly to the fact that more and more people are becoming aware of the exceptional properties of this astonishing substance.

Advantages of resin
When people first see epoxy resin, they often have questions. Listing the specific characteristics of the resin is the best method to respond to this query. The features listed below best define the solid state after solid-state curing.

could take up to a week to achieve this condition, depending on the company and product. You can frequently find precise information about the curing time on the packaging instructions for your components. The resin can seem fully cured, but the chemical transformation typically takes much longer than expected.

Once the epoxy has thoroughly dried, practically every product has the following benefits:

- Extreme resistance against abrasion.
- Superior material toughness.
- Resistant to impact (does not shatter or splinter).
- Most of the time, minimal shrinking happens when a substance changes from a liquid to a solid.
- Densities of about 1.2 grams (per cubic centimeter).
- Products of excellent quality with exceptional UV resistance.
- The vast majority of materials adhere well (for example, also on wood).
- A hot environment to reflect heat. Insulating effect on the electrical current.
- Strong acid resistance.
- The epoxy resin virtually ever splits with proper substrate preparation.
- Excellent outdoor degradation resistance.

TIP: When the liquid, high-quality epoxy resin is rarely or never flammable.

Nearly unbeatable Durability
Premium synthetic resin creates surfaces that are solid and abrasion-resistant when fully cured. Significant mechanical loads can be applied to the material without it deforming. Additionally, it is

corrosion-proof and resistant to acids. As a result, kitchen worktops are coated with high-quality epoxy resin to make them cut-resistant.

Possible Negative Effects of Epoxy Resin

Even though epoxy resins' advantages outweigh their drawbacks, there are still some drawbacks to this substance:

- Acids in large amounts can still damage epoxy resins.
- After skin contact, the raw liquid may trigger allergies or skin rashes in some persons.
- Some items may turn yellow because they are not entirely UV lightfast.
- Epoxy that has already been set is challenging.

Are synthetic resins harmful or toxic?

Ingredients in liquid resin and hardener shouldn't be applied directly to the skin. Similar to many other medications, direct skin contact may irritate the skin or trigger allergic reactions. When dealing with epoxy, I encourage you to do so in areas with good ventilation. You should also always use eye protection goggles and, if possible, a breathing mask with a filter. You must follow the safety guidelines provided by the manufacturer, which are specified on the packaging.

Precautions:

When using epoxy resin, you should practice the following safety precautions:
- Wear eye protection that shields your eyes.
- Dress in shabby attire with long sleeves and legs (or a protective suit).
- Only operate in a space that has enough airflow. Put on complete nitrile gloves.
- Putting on an air filter-integrated breathing mask.
- Avoid filling the vessel to the top when combining the ingredients because the mixture could easily spill over as it mixes.

When manufacturing epoxy resins, no significant issues or risks should develop if these fundamental guidelines are followed.

CHAPTER 05

COLORING EPOXY RESIN: HOW MAY EPOXY RESIN BE DECORATIVELY COLORED?

Epoxy resins are typically wholly transparent and colorless. As a result, casting artifacts or collectibles into them is a common practice. Additionally, translucent epoxy resin is frequently used to construct aquariums and terrariums. You could want to tint the resin for a variety of other uses.

People of all ages and professions are now dabbling in resin art, which appears to have gained enormous popularity in recent years. The resin creates various unique objects, including jewelry, cutting boards, coasters, sculptures, and even containers. However, the resin is usually straightforward, so adding color is ultimately up to you. However, how can color be added to epoxy resin? Let's examine a few epoxy resin coloring agents and how they work.

What Can be Used to Color Epoxy resin?

You will need to add a colorant, preferably when the epoxy and hardener are mixed, as epoxy resin frequently cures entirely clear. What compounds, though, can be used to color resin? Epoxy resin can be colored with alcohol ink, mic powder, food coloring, acrylic paint, resin dye, and even eyeshadow. Here is a closer look at each of these coloring substances and how they function to give your epoxy resin color.

1. Using Resin Dye

It takes a scientific technique to use epoxy dye, also known as a resin dye, to add color to your resin castings. You may easily and quickly add color to your resin creations with little effort.

If your neighborhood store doesn't have it, you can usually find it online or in most craft stores. What is the way the dye works? Contrarily, resin dyes are signed to color resin as effectively as possible, dyeing the epoxy at the molecular level rather than just saturating it.

Resin dye's main color aesthetic is opacity, even though it still enables some light to pass through liquid resin and solid castings. Without limitations like glare or magnification, the epoxy dye gives polish forms the appearance of stained glass. In light of this, resin dye might be a good option if you search for a slightly opaque tint.

2. Using Mica Powder

Mica powder is another coloring component that novice and experienced resin artists consider the proper approach to tinting resin. Stone flakes are pulverized into a thin powder to create mica powder. These powders are frequently colored and sparkly because the stones used to make them are often pigmented and shiny. Mica powder can be compared to glitter but lacks reflective qualities. When mixed with epoxy resin, mica powder spreads its color evenly.

Mica powder is completely light-opaque and creates a thick finish. This is ideal if you want to produce solid resin forms or an excellent with an excellent color finish. The enormous variety of colors that mica powder can produce is its most alluring quality. The most important aspect is that mica powder is typically inexpensive, making it possible to stock various colors in case you need to dye some epoxy resin or any other materials or surfaces that mica powder may color.

3. Using Eyeshadow Dye

Compared to other plastic composite materials, the resin is a straightforward material to color. It's simple to color your resin with some leftover eye shadow. Surprised? Since the color tone resembles adding mica powder to resin, it's a trick that knowledgeable resin artists are familiar with. Therefore I don't blame you.

All you have to do to give your resin a lovely look is to add some eyeshadow and stir it with a toothpick.

This is a practical workaround to be aware of in an emergency, and it also serves as a solid justification for purchasing some excellent eyeshadow shades. They do the job and, if necessary, can even be blended with other color agents. If you had added some mica powder, the result would have been more spectacular.

4. Using ink dye With Alcohol

Although alcohol-based ink is relatively successful at adding color to resin, due to its power, it is often not suggested for novices. Compared to other coloring ingredients, alcohol-based inks are very pigmented and offer a lot of "bang for your buck." They cannot be added to the resin and hardener as they are being combined, which makes using them for the first time challenging.

To prevent alcohol ink from interfering with the resin's initial chemical interaction with the hardener, it is best to add it while it is still curing.

After the resin has been poured into the mold or placed on the tabletop is the ideal moment to add the alcohol ink.

s a result, it can tint your resin without impacting how it bonds and cures. Resin can be colored using additional dyes. Even still, alcohol-based ink is one of the best solutions because it requires very little shade and offers a wide range of brilliant colors.

5. Using Acrylic Paint

you're an artist experimenting with resin for the first time, chances are you already have some acrylic paint on hand. The good news is that acrylic paint is one of the only graded paint for resin use because the base materials are compatible. It's important to note that acrylic paint's lack of intensity may disappoint you if your goal is to make your resin "pop" with color.

Why? Due to the paint's frequent use of resin castings to create swirls and an overall impression of movement, the color's intensity isn't powerful.

High-quality acrylic paints typically offer a brighter color than those you can pay less for, though this relies on the type of acrylic paint you are dealing with. Because there are so many colors and brands to choose from, you may choose a tint and finish for any occasion when coloring your resin castings with acrylic paint.

6. Using Glitter

Glitter may be used for much more than the occasional birthday card or party decoration, so if the mood strikes, you might add some to your resin casts to give them color. Even though glitter rarely adds color, if you use enough, your resin workpieces can gain from cat a fraction of the cost of most of the coloring techniques we've discussed thus far.

Selecting the proper type of glitter is crucial because the wrong kind will sink to the bottom of your container. Finer glitter dust can be mixed with resin to ensure that your color is applied evenly because it will stay suspended within the resin.

The benefit of utilizing glitter is that you may create works of art in multiple colors, combine various shades of glitter dust and add them to your resin before or during the casting process for an utterly stunning appearance.

Using this technique, you can color epoxy with minimal mess and use glitter that might sit unused in your supply cabinet for years.

Processing of Epoxy Resin

In addition to the resin and hardener, you will need additional equipment and supplies to process epoxy resin. Here, I have provided you with a summary of the most crucial ones.

Mixing smaller quantities of epoxy resin

There are specialized cups with measurement scales for use in epoxy resin art or other applications requiring small amounts of resin. The use of spatulas with a straight edge is also advised.

Mixing larger quantities of epoxy resin

Use a large container and a drill attachment with an emotional attachment to swirl the mixture for several minutes if you want to combine more than one liter of resin and hardener at once.

Drill epoxy resin

Drilling is difficult with epoxy resin because it is difficult. Choosing the right drill is essential for creating suitable holes. You have a choice of two materials, depending on numbering places and the budget you have available:

- HSS: High-performance, high-speed steel is a more inexpensive option for drilling holes in epoxy resin. However, after just a few drillings, the material turns dull.
- HM: Tungsten carbide drills comprise 90% tungsten carbide and 10% cobalt. This increases their hardness and resistance to temperature while also making them slightly more fragile. Therefore, tungsten carbide drills are much better for frequent use or drilling multiple holes.

Sanding Epoxy Resin

You can wet sand epoxy resin or dry sand it. Sanding with dampness is frequently carried out by hand because wetness can cause short circuits in electric sanders. You'll need a wet sanding block and a hard rubber sanding block. The surface is sanded in circular motions, from coarse to fine grain. This method can be used on arp edges, such as those on tables composed of epoxy resin.

Polishing epoxy resin

Depending on the form, texture, and resin used, the resin's surface may appear slightly rough and matte after application. This is where polishing the surface can help. Using a polishing machine and an appropriate polishing paste for larger surfaces is advisable.

With this, the epoxy resin can be easily polished to a high-gloss surface according to your preferences. To manufacture smaller objects like resin jewelry or casting molds while keeping both hands free, utilize a drill and drill stand. You have complete control over the polishing procedure thanks to this.

UV Resin Processing

A unique resin called UV Resin becomes rigid when exposed to UV radiation. The best way to cure it with a UV light or UV torch because the sun doesn't shine strongly enough and frequently enough at our latitudes. As a result, the epoxy resin may be treated very fast, and the UV resin has already begun to solidify after one to two minutes.

Epoxy Resin is poured using Silicone Molds.

Epoxy resin can be painted, used as a coating material, and poured into molds to produce three-dimensional things. There are numerous options, ranging from geometric forms and coasters to more sophisticated shapes and jewelry.

Many silicone molds are available, and epoxy resin casting is best accomplished with these molds. After hardening, you may easily mold the item by covering the mold with non-adhesive silicone. If you want to create silicone molds, replicating silicone simplifies the process.

Remove the Epoxy Resin

You will quickly discover that removing epoxy glue is not that simple if you ever need to. Removal of the casting resin after it has been set has been accomplished using a hot air dryer and a scraper. Isopropyl alcohol or vinegar is appropriate if the resin is still liquid.

What Distinguishes Liquid Resin Dye from Pigment Powder?

The easiest ways to tint epoxy are liquid resin dye and pigment powder (similar to mica powder). On the other hand, their approaches to coloring resin differ just a little. Pigment powder is a mixture of innumerable small tiny casting cast the resin color.

Due to its homogeneous distribution throughout the casting's interior volume, the resin seems to have the same shade as the powder. Both are liquid dyes that produce solutions diluted in resin; it then acquires the dye's hue. But the way that liquid resin dye and alcohol-based inks operate is different.

Dyeing is excellent, but unlike pigment powder, dyes tend to fade over time when exposed to direct sunshine, which is unfortunate because castings tinted with liquid resin dye look beautiful outside.

Due to their lower susceptibility to UV deterioration, pigment powders undergo substantially less decomposition than resin dyes, which is what you want if you use epoxy resin to create items like baby mobiles or wind chimes. This demonstrates that the question you ask most frequently is What to Color Resin With, not How to Color Resin.

When choosing a coloring agent for your resin, consider the location of your workpiece, the resin you'll be using, and the pressures acting on it.

How to Color Epoxy Resin

It is all well and good to know what an excellent product looks like, but what counts most is learning how to color epoxy resin with it.

In light of this, we've produced a brief tutorial explaining how to apply liquid and pigment dyes to resin. When using dyes to resin castings for the first time, go carefully to get a sense of the strength of the dye and how to make your resin lighter or darker.

Get your resin ready.

Combine your resin and hardener in a 1:1 ratio for consistency. By doing this, you may prevent resin from being either excessively fluid or too lumpy. To ensure that you can always see the color of your resin and the quantity you have on hand, I advise performing this technique in a clear container.

Using Pigment Powder

When compared to alternative techniques for applying epoxy colors, utilizing pigment powder is simple and enjoyable. Wears a mask and some gloves to avoid inadvertently breathing in the fine pigment powder that is there and can get everywhere.

Add the Powdered Pigment.
Add the color confident when you are sure that the resin and hardener have been appropriately combined. I advise using a small spoon and filling it to the brim with pigment powder before adding it to your resin container.

Using a mixing stick, stir the resin and pigment powder combination until the powder begins to bind to the resin mixture. As you combine, the color should change.

Add extra color dye to the container if you're unhappy with the intensity. When is the resin ready, and how can you tell? Once the color powder and epoxy resin have been thoroughly combined, there shouldn't be any powdery residue left in the container.

How To Use Liquid Resin Dye

Using liquid dye may have a high learning curve for beginners, but as long as you are cautious and watchful, it shouldn't be too difficult. Utilizing liquid pigments for epoxy resin gives you great value for your money because they create vibrant color palettes for epoxy colors.

Get your resin ready.
Before pulling out your liquid dye, you need resin to color. In a clear container, combine your resin and hardener. This will enable you to keep an eye on the resin's color and consistency as you add the dye.

To achieve the ideal consistency before adding the liquid color, ensure your resin has been diluted exactly 1:1.

Add Your Liquid Resin Dye
Get a pair of sharp scissors and remove the sealer cap typically found behind the twist-on/off caps that are included with liquid dyes. Please ensure the container's snout is pointing upward, and avoid squeezing it when you remove the safety cover. After the cap has been successfully removed, combine the resin and dye in a bowl.

Working gradually and slowly is critical in this situation. Squeeze out the tiniest quantity and mix it into the resin container. As you combine the resin and dye, observe how the color changes. Continue adding paint until the containers are the desired shade. Always start with a modest amount because once resin color is applied, it can't be taken out, meaning you'll have to start over if you put more than you told.

's time to put your newly acquired knowledge to the test. Knowing the differences between igment powders and liquid dyes and the best product for each color, you should go out and put our knowledge to the test. When dealing with resin, always wear gloves and a face mask, and make sure your workspace is sufficiently ventilated.

CHAPTER 06
EPOXY RESIN SAFETY PRECAUTION

Entropy Epoxy Resins: Safe Handling

Working with epoxy will become more enjoyable, fulfilling, and safe with the help of these safety measures for epoxy resin. Although most epoxy-related health issues are minor, I want you to have no problems. The good news is that avoiding these issues with a few precautions is simple.

The risks associated with using epoxy resins made by Entropy Resins will be discussed, along with some typical shop risks. Follow the common sense guidelines to protect your security, efficiency, and pleasure from the extraordinary and spectacular things you can create using Entropy Resins.

Topics Of Epoxy Resin Safety Precautions

- Why you should prevent Overexposure: Overexposure prevention
- Working Clean
- Disposing of Epoxy Safely.
- Epoxy-related Hazards

Why You Should Prevent Overexposure

The majority of chemicals have a safe exposure threshold. The overexposure threshold of a chemical is reached faster, the more hazardous it is. Health issues are brought on by exposure levels that are too high. Your immune system and general health may impact your ability to tolerate a chemical.

The Entropy Resins product line's epoxy resins and hardeners are created with the best physical qualities while posing the fewest environmental and human health risks. This keeps the number of dangerous substances in these products at a level where you can easily avoid overexposure using sensible work practices.

Hazardous compounds can enter the body through ingestion, inhalation, or skin absorption. The usual route of a chemical depends on its physical characteristics and everyday uses.

Epoxy Hardeners And Resins

When liquid, resin, hardener, and combined epoxy are more susceptible to exposure. Epoxy interacts chemically to form a solid as it dries or cures. Sanding dust, which we'll talk about next, is the only other possible route by which solidified epoxy could enter the body.

Skin contact is the most frequent method of exposure to resins and hardeners. Minor skin-to-skin contact that occurs frequently can provide health. Occasionally, hazardous substances may be absorbed through prolonged or recurrent skin contact.

Exposure through inhalation is uncommon because epoxy resins have a sluggish rate of evaporation. However, this risk rises if you are heating the epoxy, working in a confined space, or if your workspace is not adequately ventilated.

Epoxy Dust That Has Partially Cured

Epoxy that hasn't thoroughly dried when sanded emits airborne particles that can get on your skin, in your mouth, or get breathed. The epoxy may take up to two weeks to properly cure, even though it can be filed after only a few hours. It's possible that the epoxy dust still has hazardous components present that haven't yet reacted. Never undervalue or disregard this sanding risk.

Effects of Epoxy Exposure on Health

Let's examine the most typical health issues related to epoxy use. We can almost all steer clear of these problems. Even people with health difficulties can typically continue using epoxy with a few extra precautions.

Dermatitis

Less than 10% of people exposed to too much epoxy resin or hardener respond. A severe case of dermatitis is the typical outward sign of the reaction. Rashes may develop after using epoxy resin or hardener. Even the discomfort could be terrible; symptoms usually fade once adhesive contact is broken. On the other hand, constant contact may result in contact dermatitis.

Typically, this is milder but lasts longer. It may involve swelling, blisters, and itching and can develop into eczema if not treated over an extended length of time. Contact dermatitis can also result from sanding dust from partially-cured epoxy that collects on the skin.

Allergic dermatitis (Sensitization)

Less than 2% of epoxy users will experience allergic dermatitis, a more severe condition brought on by the body overreacting to an allergen. Sensitization, a type of allergy, emerges after repeated exposure. The strength and frequency of your epoxy exposure, immune system, and risk of getting allergic dermatitis are all factors.

You will be more susceptible if you have already developed an allergy to an epoxy chemical or have been seriously overexposed to epoxy. Fair skin, prior exposure to other sensitizing chemicals, hay fever or other allergies, or stress all raise the risk.

Epoxy might make you sensitive after several exposures or only one. Some people become hypersensitive in just a few days, while others may take years. Since there is no way to estimate how much exposure you can withstand before developing an allergy, the best action is to prevent all disclosure. Epoxy allergies can cause skin rashes or breathing difficulties. Skin irritation is by far the most frequent side effect.

It frequently has a poison ivy appearance and can cause swelling, itching, and red eyes. The symptoms may be sudden or chronic and may be moderate to severe. Your respiratory system may become irritated if you inhale epoxy vapors regularly or for extended periods.

Chemical Burns and Severe Irritation

On their own, many epoxy hardeners have a mild caustic flavor. Burns caused by hardeners are uncommon, whereas burns caused by mixed epoxy are sporadic. If hardener comes into touch with the skin, it can cause significant chemical burns and severe skin irritation. These gradually manifest and start as little pain and irritability. The burn may leave a faint scar on the skin.

The area of the skin and the hardener concentration determine how quickly epoxy hardener will burn the skin. Hardener is less corrosive because of the dilution caused by mixing it with resin. While mixed epoxy is less corrosive than pure epoxy, Never let it sit on your skin since it quickly hardens and is difficult to remove.

Respiratory Anxiety

The epoxy vapor that has been significantly concentrated has the danger of irritating and sensitizing the lungs. At room temperature, epoxy vapor concentrations shouldn't be too high. However, even to little amounts of vapor can cause an allergic reaction if you already have an allergy to epoxy. Epoxy vapor concentrations rise in hotter environments and without adequate ventilation.

Sanding epoxy before it has fully cured might have detrimental effects on one's health. When stuck in the mucus lining of your respiratory system after inhaling, epoxies chemical particles can cause excruciating itching and respiratory allergies. Epoxy chemicals are reactive until they have been cured.

Preventing Excessive Epoxy Exposure

General Epoxy Resin Safety Instructions & Precautions

These recommendations cover both professional and recreational epoxy use. They'll shield you against epoxy and other dangerous substances if you follow them.

- Use the product that will complete the task with the fewest risks. This lessens or even gets rid of the sources of danger.

- Create a secure store. Install safety measures and adhere to protocols to avoid or decrease exposure. Adequate ventilation comprises everything from low-tech floor or window fans to sophisticated air-filtration and exhaust systems, depending on your workshop. This applies to a variety of gases and dust. Exposure can be decreased by designating a specific cabinet or separate space for storing hazardous materials.

- Wear protective gear for the project, such as respirators, gloves, safety glasses, goggles, and protective clothing. Gloves, eye protection, and protective gear are a must when working with epoxy. A respirator with an organic vapor cartridge will protect you against epoxy vapors. A dust/mist mask or respirator provides the best respiratory defense against noxious dust, wood dust, and epoxy dust.

Minimize Exposure to Epoxy Resins and Hardeners

The US government has not established any exposure limitations on the epoxy resins made by Entropy Resins. These guidelines are based on the appropriate dosages for the raw components I use in my formulations, as specified in the SDS for each product.

Avoid Using Epoxy Products on Your Skin

- Avoid getting resin, hardeners, mixed epoxy, and sanding dust from uncured epoxy in your eyes or on your skin. When working with epoxies, wear safety gear such as gloves and jackets. Remove any resin, hardener, or mixed epoxy that may have accidentally come into contact with your skin. Use a waterless skin cleaner to remove resin or mixed epoxy from your skin because the resin is not water-soluble. You can remove hardeners from your skin by washing them with soap and warm water because they are soluble.

- After using epoxy, including sanding, wash your hands thoroughly with soap and warm water. If epoxy gets on your clothes, you should replace them right away. To get epoxy off your skin and clothes, use skin cleaners. Wearing garments with epoxy on it is not recommended. If the item is mixed with epoxy, you can re-wear it after it has fully hardened.

- Avoid using solvents to attempt to remove epoxy from your skin. The chemicals in the epoxy can penetrate your skin when exposed to solvents, even safe ones like vinegar, increasing the likelihood of overexposure.

- If you get a response, stop applying the epoxy. Work should only be resumed until symptoms subside, typically after several days. When you consistently avoid lengthy exposure to epoxy, its fumes, and sanding dust, improve your epoxy safety precautions.
- Stop using the drug and see a doctor if the problems persist.

Protect Your Vision and Eyes

- Protect your eyes from resin, hardeners, mixed epoxy, and sanding dust by wearing safety glasses or goggles.
- If epoxy unintentionally gets in your eyes, rinse them immediately with low-pressure water for 15 minutes. Obtain medical help.

Protect your respiratory system and lungs.

- Prevent inhaling epoxy vapors and sanding dust. All epoxies have minimal volatile organic contents (VOC). However, fumes can still build up in closed spaces. In small workshops or other restricted areas, provide enough ventilation.
- If you cannot adequately ventilate your workspace, use a respirator with an approved organic vapor cartridge.
- Wear a dust/mist mask or respirator and allow adequate ventilation when sanding epoxy, especially partially-cured epoxy. Sensitization risk is increased when epoxy dust that hasn't

thoroughly dried is inhaled. Even when the epoxy has hardened sufficiently to be sanded, may take more than two weeks to cure at room temperature fully.

Do not ingest epoxy

- Wash your hands well after using epoxy, particularly before eating or smoking.
- If you unintentionally ingest epoxy, drink much water but resist the urge to vomit. Hardene are corrosive and can get worse if you vomit them. Contact Poison Control or a doctor righ away. Consult the SDS for the product for first aid instructions.

Work Clean

- Maintain order in your workshop to avoid accidental contact with the epoxy resin. Avoi touching doorknobs, light switches, and epoxy containers if your gloves have epoxy residu since you might feel them again after removing them.
- Use a scraper to remove epoxy spills and gather as much debris as possible. Utilize pape towels afterward.
- To control large spills, use absorbent materials like sand, clay, or other neutral substances. T absorb hardeners, AVOID using sawdust or other fine cellulose materials. Reclaim pure resin c hardener for your use.
- Acetone, lacquer thinner, or alcohol are good cleaners or mixers for epoxy. Observe all safet instructions on solvent container labels.
- Hardeners shouldn't be thrown away in garbage cans with sawdust or other fine cellulos materials since they could catch fire.
- Use warm, soapy water to remove any remaining hardener.

Safety Measures for Epoxy Resin Disposal

- Puncture the can's corner to release the resin or hardener's residue into a fresh container.
- Resins and hardeners should never be disposed of as liquids. Waste resin and hardener shoul be combined in small amounts and allowed to cure into an inert solid.

CAUTION! Epoxy curing pots can heat up to the point where they release dangerous gases and ignite neighboring combustible things. Put containers of mixed epoxy away from construction sites and flammable items in a well-ventilated area. After the solid epoxy mass has thoroughly cooled and hardened, you dispose of it. Observe any municipal, state, or federal disposal laws.

Epoxy-related hazards

Uncontrolled Epoxy Curing

Exothermic chemical reactions that produce heat are used to cure epoxy. Epoxy can heat up to th point where it melts plastic, burns your skin, or sets adjacent combustibles on fire if left to heal in small area, like a mixing pot. An epoxy mass produces more heat, the more significant or thickens hundred is. One hundred grams of mixed epoxy can weigh up to 400 grams.

Pour the combined resin and hardener into a roller pan or another wide, shallow container to prever heat accumulation. Epoxy should be applied in multiple thin layers instead of one thick one whe filling vast spaces. Heat buildup and uncontrolled curing are rare in bonding and coating applications because spreading the epoxy into thinner layers dissipates heat.

Hazardous gasses like carbon monoxide, nitrogen oxides, ammonia, and probably certain aldehydes are created as the combined resin and hardener thermally decompose. When warmed, such as using a flame to remove a cast or an implanted object, these gases are cured overheated. Work in an area with good ventilation, and only use a flame as a last resort. Set the container aside where you can keep an eye on it while the remaining mixed epoxy cures. Vapors can be spread out and directed away from people using a fan. Respirators that purify the air might not be sufficient for these vapors and gases.

A fire may start if hardeners are mixed with sawdust, woodchips, or other cellulose. Heat is produced when the hardener is poured on top of or combined with sawdust due to the amine's reaction with the air and moisture. This can ignite the sawdust if it is not extinguished soon. Never attempt to clean up a hardener spill using sawdust or other cellulose material. Don't put hardener that hasn't been utilized in a garbage bin alongside cellulose items like sawdust.

Periodic Entropy Since epoxy resins and hardeners have flash points of more than 200°F (93°) and disperse slowly; they are categorized as non-flammable chemicals. In the presence of epoxy fumes, furnaces, wood stoves, and other heat sources do not provide a significant fire risk.

Spraying epoxy

Epoxy spraying carries significant dangers to one's health and safety. Hence I never advise it. AA little mist of epoxy is released from a spray gun nozzle, making it too easy to breathe in. Other health issues, as well as severe lung damage, may result from this. Your skin may become sensitized and experience an allergic reaction if this mist settles on it. Your eyes could become injured if it determines there.

Compared to other application methods, spraying releases more dangerous volatile components. Health and safety issues increase when solvents are used to thin the epoxy. The flammability and health risks are the same as any spray painting job. You can reduce dangerous vapor and mist when spraying epoxy by using isolation and enclosure, such as a ventilated and filtered spray booth. Wear a respirator that delivers air and full-body protective clothing at all times.

Removing Unused Hardener And Epoxy

Follow these steps to dispose of any leftover resin and hardeners properly.

- Save any leftover resin and hardeners for upcoming projects to reduce waste. When kept in sealed containers, epoxy materials from Entropy Resins have a long shelf life.
- Unwanted resin and hardener should be combined before allowing the mixture to dry and cool to a non-hazardous solid.
- Draining is more superficial in warm vessels.
- Attempt to empty the container owing away any empty resin or hardener containers. At the time of disposal, the container's inside should contain no more than 3% of its total weight.

- Recover any uncontaminated epoxy that has been spilled or leaked. It is waste if it is polluted. If you clean up a spill with solvent, the contaminated epoxy-solvent mixture may be considered a controlled hazardous waste.
- Do not ever release hazardous waste into the air, water, or ground. Many localities organize periodic waste collections and accept domestic waste for proper disposal.
- The preceding disposal recommendations might not align with your location's rules and ordinances. Consult your local, state, and federal laws if you're unsure.

Epoxy Safety Overview

You are responsible for your health and safety. By being knowledgeable about the items you use, following the safety instructions for epoxy resin, and adopting shop safety precautions, you can safeguard your health and safety when utilizing Entropy Resins epoxy products. Each Entropy Resins product label has the necessary hazard warnings and safety instructions.

CHAPTER 07
EASY RESIN CRAFT TO MAKE AT HOME

Incredible Resin Art Ideas You Won't Believe Are Doable at Home

Combining epoxy resin and hardener produces a stunning, rock-solid finish over nearly any material. Even though the resin is simple to work with, preparation is essential. Set up your workspace and equipment before mixing the first batch. A dust-free room or garage (preferably 65°F-70°F) should have heavy-duty plastic covering the floors and work surface.

Use disposable cups and stir sticks for simple cleanup, and wear old clothes and latex gloves. For flat tasks like artwork, you should also have a level on hand to ensure that the resin distributes evenly. It's time to play now that your room is ready, starting with easy tasks like coasters and glossy artwork. You'll have enough resin because most packages are large enough to use for several projects.

1. Glossy Impact

Easy art may be created with art paper, a canvas, and resin mixture, like the enormous succulent in this wall gallery. Attach art paper to a canvas, such as this 10x10 Inch Wrapped Canvas, while working on a level, safe surface.

More decoupage medium should be applied to the paper, smoothing out any air bubbles and letting dry. Use your finger to round the edges after pouring the clear resin into the center and allowing it to flow down the sides of the sculpture. Give the artwork 24 hours to dry. To prevent dust from gathering on the artwork's surface, I advise placing a big box or plastic tub over it.

2. Rocky Coast

These simple-to-make coasters resemble split geodes and are the ideal introduction to resin painting. Using a glue gun and glue sticks, pipe the contour of a rock shape onto a silicone mat to create a form for each coaster. When building up the edge, add some more layers and, if you lik[e] some rocks and glitter.

When dry, combine a few drops of purple, gold, blue, and white acrylic paint in each cup of clear resi[n] swirling to ensure a uniform tint. Pour a small amount of one color in the center and then repeat wit[h] the remaining shades to create the appearance of rings. The colors will spread and meld. Add som[e] sparkle.

Finish with the white paint, giving it a swirled appearance using a stir stick, then use a heat gun t[o] melt the color and remove air bubbles. To protect your furniture, line the bottoms with felt and pai[nt] the edges with gold metallic paint after giving them 24 hours to cure.

3. **Making Waves**

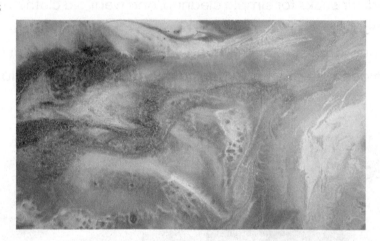

Resin mix, a blank artist canvas (ours is 24 x 24 inches), and a few craft paints produce resin art th[at] is so beautiful you can almost hear the waves breaking. Combine resin with a few drops of each [of] the following paint colors, using a different plastic cup for each color: The colors used are deep blu[e,] teal, light blue, and white with some clear resin. Utilized a total of 32 ounces of mixed resin for th[e] canvas. Pour the transparent resin into the form of a canvas's stripes or waves.

Pour the blues and teals over the canvas while moving in the same direction (and keeping the color[s] apart), blending if desired with a gloved finger. Use a heat gun to continue combining the color[s.] Sprinkle some blue or teal glitter on the canvas to make it shimmer. Spread thin white resin stripes t[o] resemble foam, using heat to combine the colors. Cover with a sizable box or tub to keep the surfac[e] free of dust as it cures flat for at least 24 hours.

Tip: To conceal drips at the canvas edge and give your DIY artwork a polished appearance, trim *with a thin frame.*

4. River Still Life

Use this simple concept to capitalize on the river rock table trend. Wash river rocks with soapy water, then allow them to air dry (or purchase a set from a crafts store). Arrange the stones inside a lamp with a glass base and a detachable top. Then, add resin to the center of the rocks, allowing them to fill in around the pebbles. Spray some polyacrylic spray on a fake flower, let it dry, and then place it over the rocks. Before utilizing the lamp, give the resin 24 hours to dry out.

5. Resin Photo Art

Use resin art to carefully preserve images in a location where you'll see them every day. Resin art isn't merely comprised of abstract designs. I utilized clear resin and a sizable family portrait to personalize this wood jewelry box. Trim your photo to fit within the resin mold of your choice to create your own, then pour and spread the resin over the surface until it is completely coated. Heat the resin using a heat gun to eliminate bubbles before allowing it to dry.

6. Cubist Design

When enclosed in resin art, dried and synthetic greenery doesn't deteriorate. Center it in the bottom of a square resin mold if you're working with a single large object (like the fake air plant and silk flower I used). Use a heat gun to reheat the resin mixture to remove bubbles before adding it to the mold.

Pour over the item and leave it for 24 hours before taking it out of the mold. Fill the mold with clear resin to the brim for smaller flowers, attach the foliage and blooms into the resin using a sharp stick, and allow it to cure.

7. Doodle Craft

Decorate a tabletop with resin drips in various colors and a marking pen. Draw natural forms like leaves, berries, and flowers to cover the surface with patterns. Use stamps or stencils instead of doodling if you lack confidence in your abilities. Filling certain portions of the way with colored resin using an artist's brush and gently tapping will give it a three-dimensional appearance.

8. Sweet Accents

Amplify the charm of commonplace items. A wooden napkin ring is given a sweet touch by a candy mold that is capped with resin and filled with sugar sprinkles.

9. Resin Buttons

In just a few simple steps, you can create your handcrafted buttons. Add buttons to sweaters, throw pillows, and other crafts to enhance the homemade look. Purchase a resin button mold, epoxy resin, polyamine hardener, and acrylic paint in the colors you like for the buttons before continuing. Add a little bit of the acrylic craft paint to the resin and mix to color. If the button holes are covered in resin, take the button from the mold when it is still rubbery (a few hours later), and insert a pin to reveal the holes. If not, wait 24 hours before removing the buttons from the mold.

10. Napkin Rings

Add resin accents to simple napkin rings. To make these chic flowers, I employed a fondant mold. To manufacture it, mix acrylic craft paint into a 1:1 mixture of epoxy resin and polyamine hardener before pouring the mixture into a rubber mold and letting it dry for 24 hours.

Remove the ornament from the mold before the resin can fully harden if you wish to curl it around the napkin ring. The flexible resin should be gently bent around the ring's curvature, hot-glued to the ring, and then let to finish drying.

11. Cabinet Knobs

Add playful flowery resin knobs cast in contact lens cases to spruce up cabinet doors. Place a piece of vintage jewelry upside down in the mold after spraying the case with mold release and adding resin. Top with a machine screw that has been put at a 90-degree angle once the resin has reached the consistency of gel (after about 20 minutes). Before removing the knob from its mold, let it dry for 24 hours. Before mounting, provide a space between the knob and the cabinet door by threading a machine nut onto the screw.

12. Door Knob

Something as straightforward as a doorknob may be given a little glitz and beauty! Add resin to complete the look of a practical concave-face doorknob in a few easy steps. To create a circle that ts the knob's curve, punch a piece of scrapbook paper to fit the knob's face and cut a slit from the edge to the middle of the article. Apply two coats of decoupage material on the doorknob after attaching the form.

fter the decoupage mixture has dried, center a beautiful ornament on the handle. Pour a 1:1 ombination of epoxy resin and polyamine hardener on top while working on a level surface. Before installing the doorknob, wait 24 hours.

13. Picture Frame

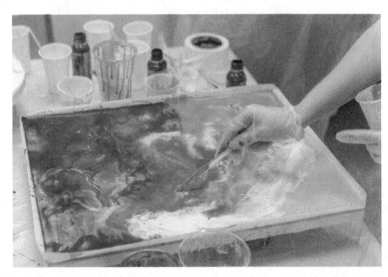

ut a particular photo on display with this simple frame. Cut off the picture. Cut a second paper circle nd attach it to the back to give the image weight. Decoupage medium is used to seal both sides; llow to dry. Spray mold release within a soap mold.

fter that, put the photo on top of the resin. Insert the picture facedown into the resin using a oothpick. Before removing the frame from the resin mold, let it for 24 hours to dry. Cut some lovely aper to fit the back of the frame, then fix it with spray glue to complete the look. Use a small easel to isplay the finished photography project.

14. Floral Paper Weight

Who would have imagined a paperweight would be valuable? Create this attractive paperweight to old errant papers on your desk or work surface. All you need to add a fashionable touch is resin, a

bowl for a mold, and dried flowers. Fill a plastic paint mixing cup with resin and top it off with mol
release. Using a toothpick, "float" dried flowers—I used dried baby's breath—at different levels in th
resin to add dimension. Before removing the paperweight from its mold, let it dry for 24 hours.

15. Suncatcher

To reflect light and color throughout the room, hang this sea glass-inspired mobile in a bright windov
To create this vibrant design, you need some resin, water-bottle ice cube trays, and a few drops c
food coloring. Epoxy resin and polyamine hardener should be poured into the rubber ice cube tray
in a 1:1 ratio. Each resin mold should have one or two drops of food coloring added before being stirre

After they have dried, take the reflectors out of the mold and screw an eye into the top of each on
The fishing line should be tied to the hooks before suspending the glasses from a metal ring at variou
heights.

CHAPTER 08
BEST RESIN CRAFT IDEAS: RESIN CRAFTING PROJECTS

What Is Resin Crafting?

Resin craftsmanship can be viewed from many angles, but what is it at its core? Construction or reproduction of forms using a variety of molds is known as resin crafting. Epoxy resin in liquid form is poured into these molds to fill them. After that, as the liquid dries and hardens, a flawless reproduction of the negative from the mold hold is created.

The idea is that resin can be used to duplicate everything found in a mold. Why would you want to do this? You might want more of a particular item, have a favorite ornament, or wish to utilize your imagination to make something unique and one-of-a-kind. Whatever your motivation, there is something for everyone in epoxy resin crafts, and there are several types of epoxy resin for various uses. Why is resin available in such wide varieties?

Several resin kinds are available for different applications since some resins are plain, others are colored, some are multicolored, and some are plastic for additional rigidity. How many uses for resin are there? The wide range of resins available is well justified when you consider that epoxy resin is employed in every aspect of modern civilization, from crafting to automotive engineering to the construction of Jewish artifacts and even tool insulation.

When Was the First Resin Made?

Although you wouldn't be entirely mistaken if you assumed that resin was a relatively recent discovery, the first synthetic resin was produced in 1909. Because it was pliable and thus versatile, the first resin iteration—Bakelite—could be utilized for thousands of diverse purposes.

Various naturally occurring resins were previously available, but they might be challenging to grow and even more difficult to work with. This is why the invention of Bakelite at the start of the 20th century marked the beginning of the "plastic" age.

You may remember the Tupperware craze of the 1970s when several homemakers and television commercials urged purchasing this innovative, cost-effective, and durable line of containers that could be used to store almost everything you could think of.

Even though there are tight restrictions governing which plastics can be used in mass manufacturing today and that this type of plastic isn't particularly beneficial for the environment, back then, firms saw dollar signs in the research and development of resin-related items.

Plastic resins are essentially a by-product of the cracking process used in oil refining. As a result of this procedure, the substance is changed into either propylene resin or ethylene resin, which can subsequently be reused, molded, colored, and sold to the general public.

Like other polymers, epoxy resin is created through a reaction between epichlorohydrin and bisphenol-A. By changing the chemical makeup of the finished plastic, several varieties of resin can be made.

Although it may appear complicated, there are several straightforward techniques to work with resin to get the desired outcome. There are countless possibilities because some materials are so powerful that they can even be used in place of metals!

In light of this, I should probably return to crafts made from epoxy resin. As we've already indicated, the resin may create various objects. However, you do not need to use the readily available molds in stores or online. If you were to make your manufacturer, you could make a mold of whatever you discover and reproduce.

Many people take advantage of this by purchasing resin mold-making kits, replicating desired forms, personalizing them, and then selling them as a hobby or side hustle. Considering what you can make with these resin mold kits with imagination and perseverance, they are accessible and reasonably priced.

Toys for kids, electronic parts for cars, jewelry, food molds, and even shoes might all be cloned! However, if you decide to go this path, Be careful not to use anyone's artwork or intellectual property without that person's permission.

What could be included in resin?

Resins can be tailored in several ways to suit your preferences. Here are some intriguing accents you may use to add personality to your epoxy resin projects. These upgrades are cheap and straightforward, but they scratch the surface of the potential.

- Glitter
- Little things
- Coloring agent
- Dyes
- Flowers

- Clothing beads
- Photographs
- Wood shavings
- Sequins

What kind of materials can you use resin on?

you use your imagination, the resin may be applied to practically any surface. When people talk about resin, they often refer to the castings you can make using the molds they come with. Here are a few daily applications for resin. It's usually a good idea to do some research on the materials you're working with because some surfaces can require extra prepping.

What Materials Can I Use Resin On?

- Metal Surface
- Wood Surfaces
- Mortar Surfaces
- Plastic Surfaces
- Canvas Backings
- Glass Surfaces
- Paper Surfaces
- Ceramic Surfaces

What Materials Can't I Use Resin On?

- Wax
- Polyurethane (PU) Surfaces
- Grease or Oil
- Silicone
- Polyethylene
- Polypropylene
- Painters Tape
- Parchment

What Kinds of Molds Are Appropriate for Resin Casting?

Molds exist in various shapes and sizes, allowing people to use them to make many incredible things. Molds can also be made from different materials, incorporating various casting materials and resin kinds. Here are a few illustrations of the other molds you might encounter during resin casting.

Plastic Molds / Store-Bought Silicone

These mold varieties are more frequently purchased. Why? Because they are simple to make and inexpensive to generate in large quantities. However, not all of them are built of recyclable materials, making them not necessarily environmentally friendly. These molds can be used to create a variety of molds that are usually seen in starting kits or children's toys. They are frequently affordable.

Since there isn't much surface friction, which would otherwise cause the resin to attach to surface, they frequently have a smooth surface. They also have the advantage of being easy to clea, allowing frequent use.

DIY Latex and Silicone Molds

You are not required to utilize the molds manufacturers sell because they come with resin an, harden. Although you do have the option of producing your molds using kits for either rubber or late the majority of people prefer the simple fun of generating unique forms.

In essence, some substances can be combined to create a particular kind of putty that can duplicat a form by leaving a negative imprint. This was the standard procedure for reproducing objects resin before 3D printing, and plastic molds were invented.

Prepare and shape the mold-making materials around the item you want to copy; remove the silicone or latex of the object after allowing it to dry for the amount of time recommended by the manufacturer. You are now prepared to begin making resin castings.

Which Projects for Resin Crafting Are Best for You?

It would take a very long time to list everything made of resin. Check out a few resin crafts project that you can finish in two to three hours instead, whether you're working on them alone, with friend or with family.

1. Resin Tabletop

If you enjoy DIY home improvements, this is a great first project. You can utilize resin tabletops to add essential aesthetic touches to your house or go all out and construct something unique. The experience will be a ton of fun in either scenario! Before you start, gather the following materials: a tabletop, a base coat, the resin colors you want to show up in your workpiece, a paintbrush, a heat gun or blowtorch, a short PVC pipe, and several cups to mix them in.

The first step is to blend and apply the base coat of resin to your tabletop. Depending on the resin colors you have chosen, this color may either stand out sharply or blend in beautifully. After the foundation layer has been put in place, use a paintbrush to evenly and flushly apply the resin to the surface and let it dry.

Use a blow torch or heat gun to eliminate bubbles and expedite drying. Combine the various resin colors in their cups once they have dried. After blending the colors, place the PVC pipe on the table and pour the pigments into the cylinder.

Slide the cylinder in the desired pattern after they have been poured in to finish creating your tables. Apply the final clear coat on your piece of art after the resin has dried, then take in the beauty of it.

2. Resin Jewelry

This is one of the unique venues for beginners to start their resin casting experience. When it comes to jewelry casting, there are a ton of creative paths you may go down, and the most significant part is that you can wear your creations later on! Jewelry castings are simple to create and straightforward to find their molds. If you went to the store to buy one, you would undoubtedly find that jewelry resin molds are sold in packs of multiple molds.

Hair clips, rings, earrings, bracelets, necklaces, and even chokers are standard accessories that you should be able to construct easily. This is the most straightforward resin craft for beginners because you must combine the resin and hardener before pouring the mixture into the mold of your choice.

To make your casting more appealing, add grains of rice, individual letters, glitter, or color swirls while the resin cures. Attaching a pin or chain plug is also optional. If you want that effect, you may incorporate these modifications into your resin as you combine it with the hardener. Anything you can wear technically qualifies as an accessory. As a result, endless items can be turned into jewelry using epoxy resin crafts.

3. Resin place mats and Coasters

Is there anything more advantageous than a hobby you can practice every day? The capacity to create products that can be used throughout your home is one of the characteristic aspects of renin making. Despite this, castings for placemats and coasters are some of the more popular beginner resin crafts.

Jewelry-related popular beginner resin crafts are not the only ones available. Why, if I may ask? These castings make a fantastic birthday or holiday presents for your friends and family because they are simple to manufacture and can be personalized.

The possibilities are unlimited; you could design a set of coasters or placemats using family photos, make one for each family member using their favorite color, or incorporate something special into a set of coasters to act as a constant reminder of your friends and loved ones. These molds are fantastic since they are strong, versatile, and straightforward.

If you wish to reproduce the shape of a coaster or placemat, mix your resin and hardener, pour the mixture into the mold, and let it set. Aside from the contents, keep in mind that resin may also be cut and sanded, allowing you to market your creations.

Like jewelry, coasters and placemat molds are frequently supplied in sets, giving you the extra benefit of producing multiple separate units at once. This mold is ideal for people who want to offer their houses or the items they plan to give others a personalized touch.

4. Resin Light Bulbs

frequently overlook a practical use as significant as light production when considering epoxy for crafts. Although it may sound a little absurd, the resin can be used to make light bulbs that are beautiful to look at and effective in illuminating the area around you. Given that resin is not glass and does not refract light, how is this accomplished? Well, it is simple.

just so happens that when an LED (light-emitting diode) is inserted under the lightbulb cap, crystal resin that has been molded into the shape of a lightbulb with the proper chemical composition makes a usable lightbulb! The correct shape/form of light is perfectly absorbed and reflected by crystal resin!

epoxy is frequently used for crafts as an exercise in aesthetics, and this does fill a rustic, relaxing niche that is currently very in demand. To begin with, casting like this, you don't need to be a rocket scientist. s we did with the previous castings, combine the resin and the hardener, then pour the mixture into he mold. All that's left to do is add the LED to the top of the dried-out light bulb casting, remove it om the mold, add the lightbulb cap, and you're good to go!

5. Using resin and alcohol ink together

here are hundreds, if not thousands, of resin crafting ideas accessible, but some might get more ifficult the further you go down the rabbit hole. If you're searching for a quick and simple trick, try dding alcohol ink to your resin casting.

What distinguishes alcohol ink from ordinary ink? Consider the impact of resin dye and regular ink as eing more subdued than their alcohol counterpart on a casting. Alcohol ink is frequently used with rystal resin because it enhances the resin type's overall glassy appearance. Additionally, it istinguishes itself from other coloring agents by preserving the resin's clarity.

Alcohol ink's key selling point is that it keeps the resin translucent after the added dye. This ndicates that you may achieve the same result by mixing a small amount of this ink with a clear resin, which is a little less expensive than colored resin.

Because it is affordable and can produce some intriguing effects, which few people are aware of many individuals prefer to employ this approach in their DIY resin projects. You may drop anything made of resin without shattering it into a million pieces. The appearance is comparable to stained glass without the hassle of dealing with such a delicate material. Consider objects like "stained glass bowls, drinkware, placemats, and coasters.

6. Resin Paintings

This isn't exactly what most people consider an "entry-level" DIY resin project, so I should start by stating that. Resin paintings are relatively new, and if you are skilled at creating them, you might be able to sell them for a reasonable price.

They can be a little challenging to create outside of the commercial market. Painting requires considerable talent (any fine art); however, working with a medium like resin can be frustrating if you don't have the correct temperament. Please persevere; resin painting can be enjoyable, a great way to express oneself, and an excellent indicator of the creator's attitude.

Their best feature is that designs made with resin on canvas or another surface are frequently surprisingly good. It could take one or two tries to get the hang of things if you're trying to construct anything specific. It can be expensive to purchase resin in the numbers required to create paintings of a standard size, but this doesn't preclude you from making a smaller piece of art specifically for you.

A peaceful afternoon alone with your thoughts and a lot of resin and hardener in the colors of your choice could be seen as rewards in and of themselves.

To ensure that the paint is permanently kept, you can add a glossy clear coat after you finish. Using a blowtorch or heat gun is preferable on the workpiece's surface. Could you make sure there are no bubbles in it?

7. Using resin to fill wood voids

Most resin enthusiasts like this process, but it could be daunting if you don't know what you're doing. There's a strong possibility that if you have a Pinterest account, you've seen resin used in this manner.

Before resin became available to people like us, hardwood tables with sizable parts missing or that had merely deteriorated over time were thrown in the trash.

Some people may have recently spotted intentionally removing pieces of their larger tables to fill them with colorful resin. Is this decent? Is it important?

No, I don't believe that at all. The end effect is impressive and even somewhat strengthens the table. It might take a little longer than a weekend to accomplish this. Just pour the resin into the cracks. That sounds easy. Before you can start running, you must first make sure your surface is level and sand it to make it flush. Additionally, ensure you choose the right color combination and have enough resin to give the impression of flow.

Since this void filling needs a significant amount of resin, I suggest starting with a smaller workpiece and increasing your level over time. For the whole family, especially on larger projects, filling gaps with wax is a fun way to give old furniture new life.

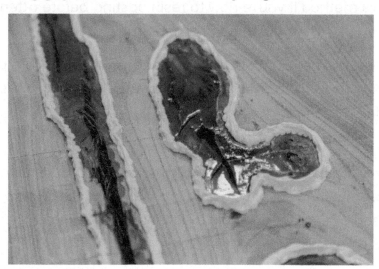

How Are Resin Castings Made?

Even the simplest castings might be frightening if you have never worked with resin before, even if knowing what you can make with resin is excellent. You can use the following tips to ensure your resin workpieces' creation goes as quickly as possible. It would help if you worked in a well-ventilated area when mixing and pouring your resin and hardener since resin is hazardous once it has hardened.

Set Up Your Work Area

Working with resin may be dirty, regardless of whether you create large or little casings. Setting up your workspace is essential since, once the resin has set and solidified, removing it off surfaces can be difficult. You want to begin by laying out a tarp to keep any resin from coming in contact with the neighboring surfaces. To protect your hands, lips, and face, gather paper towels, gloves, and a cloth face mask.

Next, depending on the size of your workpiece and the number of colors you intend to use, prepare your mixing containers and sticks for each color. Finally, prepare your molds by slathering them in a thin layer of baby powder or anti-adhesive coatings similar to those in stores.

Mix the resin and hardener.

Time to get filthy now! F This can be a little nerve-wracking for beginners because you must mix your resin and hardener at a 1:1 ratio to produce the best resin casting results. You can experience mixing the resin and hardener and working within the mixture's pot life by beginning with small epoxy resin projects. Combining a little amount of resin and hardener to obtain a sense of the viscosity and dry time of the solution will help you determine how long you have to pour the resin before it completely cures.

Try to pour the resin and hardener together as gently as possible; this will lessen the amount of trapped air brought on by the change in the liquid's surface tension and the possibility of leaks. It's a good idea to practice this method if you're new to resin casting before attempting to remove these air bubbles from the resin later on with a torch or a heat gun.

Small resin casting projects are perfect for beginners because they let them practice working quickly and efficiently while also introducing them to working with resin, which is slightly different from working with other crafting materials.

Prepare Your Mold

You can save time by preparing for mold over a long period. Why? Most new users of resin casting discover that getting their castings out of the mold is only half the challenge. Various molds and resins have different best practices for ensuring a painless demolding process, which will prevent damage to your mold and casting during removal.

It's usual practice to use an anti-adhesive spray to prevent resin castings from sticking to their molds. To speed up the demolding process, you can quickly add other friction-reducing ingredients to the interior of the mold, such as baby powder. These are commonly available online and at the majority of merchants.

Other anti-adhesive substances shouldn't be used since they can interfere with the chemical composition of the molds you want to employ. Manufacturers may add anti-adhesive sprays explicitly designed for use with mold-specific molds.

Fill Your Mold

Even though this process is simple, there are a few tips and tricks to remember to get the most out of your resin molds and create flawless castings. Pouring resin and hardener into your mold is not sufficient. Remember that your castings may have air bubbles due to the resin's surface tension being different from the mold's, which might cause imperfections.

When using epoxy for crafts, place a small amount of resin within the mold to form a thin coating. After this layer has been run, let it settle before slowly pouring the remaining rein into the mold.

efore allowing the resin to dry, ensure the mold is tightly shut once it has been poured into it (if you have a two-part mold). If your mold has two parts, ensure the connection between them is strong and consistently upholds its integrity.

ake Off Your Cast

he molds that come with epoxy for crafts are often built to work flawlessly with them, but if you ant to use a different sort or brand of epoxy with your present molds in the future, it may be ifficult to remove the epoxy once it has been set.

s I previously mentioned, one effective way to ensure that your castings don't stick to the mold iterior during the demolding process is to apply anti-adhesive materials to the interior of the mold efore the resin is poured inside.

owever, if you are excessively forceful when extracting the casting from the mold, you risk ccidentally harming both the casting and the mold. When taking the casting from the mold, it would e beneficial to try to pop it out of the cavity rather than peel it from it. Try heating pieces of the mold your molds are difficult to work with or have weird shapes. This will cause the mold to expand and elease any casting that has been trapped inside.

It's time to put your newfound knowledge to the test now that you are aware of how resin was created, what it is made of, how to cast resin on your own, what it can be used for, which forms it can be used to create and which ones are the simplest. Always operate in a well-ventilated room, wear personal protection equipment, and make sure your workspace is appropriately covered.

CONCLUSION

A liquid substance called epoxy resin is blended with different color pigments and additives to form resin art, a blend of distinctive patterns and textures. In the unusual painting technique known as resin art, no conventional brushes, acrylic, or oil paints are used. For the new generation of creatives, it is regarded as a sophisticated painting. Ordinary artists can be distinguished from resin artists by the distinctive materials they use to create their works.

I hope you learned "what is resin art?" and found this book valuable. Try out all the techniques and tools suggested. Order a resin pack immediately to start creating something of your own. Slow and steady wins the race. Try out various pigments, colors, and creative materials. Consider posting your designs on social media if you perform well. Before beginning your epoxy resin business, always choose a quality resin art kit. Working with resin is easy and versatile. Impressive resin art is possible with general knowledge and basic skills. The possibilities for using resin in the craft are endless.

The process of creating a unique resin painting is relatively tricky and sophisticated. In addition, preparations must be made before the work can start. However, producing a resin piece of art is worthwhile for any hobby artist since the stunning end product is worth the effort. When different color pigments and additives are mixed with a fluid substance called epoxy resin, it produces a variety of distinctive patterns and textures. Epoxy resin, a synthetic material created to simulate the desirable qualities of natural resin, is used in resin art. The two components of epoxy resin are synthetic polymer resin and a hardener. A chemical reaction occurs between the components of the resin mixture, progressively hardening it (when combined with a hardener) to a solid plastic.

It can be simple to jump in without conducting any research. However, resin art has unique difficulties, and there is a lot to learn, which can be intimidating. Beginners are encouraged to practice the straightforward methods used to produce stunning resin artwork to master them eventually. Due to its unique properties and compatibility with a wide range of materials, epoxy resin offers countless creative possibilities. Depending on the size of your project and how thrifty you are when buying the necessary tools, the cost of starting to experiment with resin art will vary. The cost of your new activity increases as your ideas grow. Your imagination will thrive in this secure and simple hobby!

BONUS:
How To Resin Rocks: Guide For Beginners

Resin can be easily applied to rocks (and other embedded objects). Resin elevates embedded artwork to a whole new level. In addition to acting as an adhesive to mount your materials, it also adds a glossy sheen that accentuates the texture of your collage and compels you to reach out and touch it. – You may mount the piece of art and pour the resin right on nel! Clean and smooth edges are made possible by panels with a raised lip that helps hold resin.

Your rock collage will transform from good to stunning in 24 hours by measuring, combining, pouring, spreading, covering, and waiting.

Supplies:

- A wooden art panel measuring 12 by 12.
- Ornamental rocks.
- Epoxy resin
- A spreader, a stir stick, and a set of nitrile gloves.
- A grade.
- A measuring cup with precise measurements.
- A mixing vessel.
- A small torch, such as our Artist's Torch.
- Toothpicks.
- A container to protect your object while it cures, such as an empty cardboard box or a plastic tote with the flaps removed.

Steps:

1. Put Your Rock Collage Together.

Put together your rock collage first. Before you begin, you can either freehand your design or create creating outline into the wood panel (like we did). Use resin or a very minimal adhesive to attach your rocks to the board (resin is the most potent adhesive in the world.) Allow your collage to set and dry for at least 24 hours once all the rocks have been mounded, and your collage is finished.

TIP: Because wood is an organic object, it can have trapped air that eventually escapes as bubbles in your resin. Gas bubbles can be affected by a wide range of factors, including humidity, the type of wood used, and the degree of drying of the wood. A technique to stop bubbles is to pre-seal wood using a spray or brush-on sealer. But before resining your finished project, I always recommend testing with your specific materials so you know what effects to expect. I've had enough success with these wood panels to know that they don't need to be pre-sealed. Again, pre-sealing is always a good idea if it makes you feel more at ease.

2. Determine how much resin is required.

Enter the length and breadth of your object into an online resin Calculator to determine how much resin you'll need.

TIP: *5 oz of resin is required for a standard 1/8" coating on a 12 by 12" panel (2.5 oz resin and 2.5 oz hardener). The lip of your board should be measured because it may differ.*

3. Stir well

Measure out precisely equal amounts of resin and hardener while wearing gloves. You should stir quickly for 3 minutes while scraping the mixing bowl's sides and bottom.

4. Pour the art resin in.

Using a disposable foam brush, distribute the resin from the piece's center to the perimeter so you can work around the pebbles. Before the resin becomes too thick to spread, you'll have around 45 minutes to perform.

TIP: *Because resin makes things appear wet, it can darken natural objects like rocks, wood, and other raw materials. You can accurately predict the appearance of your products once the resin is applied if you test them first with water.*

5. Put your artist's torch to use.

Just long enough to cause the bubbles in the resin to pop, hold the flame of your Artist's Torch a few inches above the resin surface while continuously moving the torch from side to side.

6. Final inspection of your work

After burning the item, examine the resin under a light to search for missing bubbles, minute hairs, or dust, and use a toothpick to get rid of them.

7. Wrap up your Artwork

Allow your item to cure for 24 hours or until it feels solid to the touch then wrap it in plastic wrap or a cardboard box (with the flaps cut off)

8. Wait for 24 hours

You are releasing your artwork after 24 hours!

TIP: *The resin will be touch-dry after 24 hours. You can certainly hang your artwork now to enjoy it, but if you're thinking about packing it up and shipping it, give the resin at least 72 hours to fully cure before doing so.*

Which resin works best with rocks?

The type of project you are working on and the desired output will determine the best resin for rocks. Epoxy resin is an attractive option for decorative applications since it offers a clear, glossy, long-lasting, and UV radiation-resistant finish. Polyester resin is a better option for structural uses since it is more durable and flexible.

What benefits can resin have over rocks?

Compared to conventional materials, resin for rocks has several benefits, including greater strength, increased flexibility, and a smooth surface. It is a fantastic option for outdoor projects because I also more UV radiation resistant. It may also be used rapidly and is reasonably simple to deal with.

What Safety Measures Should You Implement When Using Resin for Rocks?

To shield your eyes and skin from the resin while working with resin for rocks, you should always wear safety goggles and gloves. The directions for the specific resin you are using should also be familiar to you, and you should make sure you are working in a well-ventilated location.

How to Fill Epoxy with Crushed Rock?

Jewelry makers and other crafters sometimes use epoxy resin mixed with finely crushed stone as an inlay material. The resin-stone mixture can readily fill cast or carved voids in work. When the resin dries, it looks like intricately inlaid stone. To help you obtain almost any look, from turquoise to granite, there are numerous possibilities for stone type and resin color.

Supplies You'll Need
- Sandpaper Grits of 220 and 400 for Hand Sander
- epoxy resin
- Use paper or tinfoil
- Hardener for Epoxy
- Buffer in Felt
- Toothpick
- Finished Crushed Stone

Step 1
On a sheet of paper, create a pile with the crushed stone you intend to use for your inlay. Your inlay will appear denser as there are more stones used.

Step 2
Epoxy resin and hardener in two equal portions should be applied to the paper. What you'll need to fill the hollow in your inlay should roughly be the combined volume of the two.

Step 3
To get the density of stone you want for the inlay, quickly combine the epoxy resin with a toothpick, then stir in the crushed stone.

Step 4
Use toothpicks to scrape the epoxy-stone mixture off the paper and work it into the inlay. Make sure to fill the inlaid area om bottom to top. A sufficient amount of the mixture should be added, so it

mounds just above the inlay cavity's top and extends past the cavity's edge. Any excess should be removed right away.

Step 5
Follow the manufacturer's instructions and let the epoxy completely solidify.

Step 6
Using a hand sander and 220-grit sandpaper, sand the hardened epoxy until it is flat with the surface of the inlaid piece.

Step 7
Change to 400-grit sandpaper and smooth off the epoxy.

Step 8
Apply a felt buffing wheel to the epoxy and buff it to a high luster.

Tip: A more excellent range of color effects can be achieved by adding epoxy colorants or colored caulk dust to the epoxy. Choose your stone's texture based on the size of your inlay. You can use stone chips to cover a sizable area. It would be best to use incredibly tiny stone fragments for fine jewelry.

Cautions
When working with two-part epoxy, always employ adequate ventilation. Avoid letting epoxy dry out on your skin. It is preferable to combine less epoxy than not enough. After the initial inlay has dried, adding more epoxy to fill the space will leave noticeable fractures and seams.

Conclusion

There are numerous varieties of resin on the market right now, which makes it challenging to fin resin of high quality. Resin can be easily applied to rocks (and other embedded objects). Embedde artwork is brought to a whole new level by resin. You must expect beautiful things to enhance you rock's beauty. We sincerely hope you found this to be both educational and useful.

How to Make Resin Gems
How to Make a Resin Geode?

I can assure you that manufacturing these wonderful small gems couldn't be easier or more enjoyable if you require resin gems for jewelry making, crafting, or decorating. And the best part is that finding the materials you need to construct them is simple. You can have a mountain of gems at your disposal with just some resin, a mold, and extras like glitter. Here are various methods to create beautiful jewels and spice up your upcoming creative project.

Using UV Resin to Create Gems

UV Resin is the best option if you need these gems quickly or want instant gratification. Instead of the 24 hours that 2-part epoxy resins require to cure, this resin uses a UV light to cure, allowing you to have jewels ready for use in only a few minutes. Even though UV resin is more expensive, it is worthwhile if speed is of the essence.

Materials Used
- UV Resin Kit from Mr. Resin
- UV Light Curing (mine came with the above kit)
- Paxcoo Resin Molds for Making Jewelry
- Rubber Mixing Cup (Came with Mr. Resin Kit)
- Craft Sticks or Silicone Stirring Instruments
- LEOBRO 16-Color Epoxy Resin Mica Powder
- Glitter (For the opal-appearing gem, use giant flake glitter).
- Large Glitter Flakes.

Optional:
- The Silicone Work Mat
- Tweezers

Plain Clear Gem
1. Put together your work area and put in your UV lamp. Then, fill the gem mold of your choice with UV resin. Don't overfill the mold, please.
2. Verify that the resin has reached all of the corners.
3. Pop any bubbles on the resin's surface with your grill lighter or heat gun.
4. Turn on the lamp, then position it above the gem mold. Depending on how thick the resin is, this could take a while.
5. Turn the mold over and continue curing it from the front after curing from the rear.
6. Test the resin to determine if it is sticky or soft after the light has gone out. Remove it from the mold if it is challenging.

7. You can put the gem under UV light if it seems slimy to the touch. If you contact it when it's sticky, fingerprints will be left on your finished product.

Ruby Red Gem

1. Add enough resin to the little mixing cup to fill the mold's gem holes however often you want to.
2. A little bit of the red mica powder, added to the mixing cup, will go a long way. Stir to combine the color thoroughly.
3. Verify that the resin has reached all of the corners.
4. Pop any bubbles on the resin's surface with your grill lighter or heat gun.
5. Turn on the lamp, then position it above the gem mold. Depending on how thick the resin is, this could take a while.
6. Turn the mold over and continue curing it from the front after curing from the rear.
7. Test the resin to determine if it is sticky or soft after the light has gone out.
8. Remove it from the mold if it is challenging can put the gem back under the UV light if it seems slimy to the touch. If you contact it when it's sticky, fingerprints will be left on your finished product.
9. Put your silicone mixing cup under your UV light to cure and clean it. The mess can then be obliterated from the cup.

Note: It is advisable to use tiny amounts of colorants when combining them with glitters. Adding too much can prevent your item from curing, leaving you with a runny middle and an outside shell.

Add-in Gems

1. One of the gem molds should have UV resin squeezed into the bottom of it. Just enough should be added to cover the mold's bottom.
2. Add some small embellishments (I used tiny heart-shaped glitter embellishments) while ensuring they are where you want them to be with your tweezers.
3. Turn on the UV lamp and place it over the mold; let it on for roughly 45 seconds.
4. To finish filling the mold, add additional UV resin.
5. Any resin bubbles on the surface can be popped using a grill lighter.
6. Under the UV light, totally cured.

Glitter Gem

1. One of the gem molds should have UV resin squeezed into the bottom of it. Just enough should be added to cover the mold's bottom.
2. Add some glitter on top of the resin in the mold (I used some bright, opaque, white large flake glitter to make it look like opal). Push the glitter just a little bit into the resin using your tweezers.
3. Turn on the UV lamp and place it over the mold; let it on for roughly 45 seconds.
4. To finish filling the mold, add additional UV resin.
5. Any resin bubbles on the surface can be popped using a grill lighter.

6. Under the UV light, totally cured.

Note: Another way to make this is to combine the resin and glitter in the cup, then pour the mixture into the mold and allow it to set. It does have a slightly different impact as a result. You can determine which you prefer after trying both.

You may go wild with making these gems because it is a delightful and simple pastime. See what magnificent little beauties you can make by using your creativity and experimenting with different colors, glitters, and additives.

Producing Resin Gems using 2 Part Epoxy Resin

Materials Used

- ARTISAN RESIN Kit for Epoxy Resin.
- Paxcoo Resin Molds for Making Jewelry.
- Blending Cups (One for plain and one for each color).
- Craft Sticks or Silicone Stirring Instruments.
- Glitter: Small or large glitter is acceptable. Here is some glitter in a large flake form.
- Grill lighter.

Optional:

- The Silicone Work Mat
- Tweezers
- The Timer

Instructions:

1. Set up your workspace, wear gloves, and don your safety glasses. Make sure you have easy access to all of your supplies.
2. Combine a craft stick and resin in a small cup as directed on the packaging. It would be best if you used an accurate timer to time this. (When you are mixing and your hand starts to pain, time moves more slowly.) It would be best to combine this in small batches unless you work exceptionally quickly because your workday will only be between 30 and 45 minutes long.
3. Once the resin is blended, you may pour some of it into the silicone molds that are fashioned like jewels to create clear gems. Don't fill the mold with too much material. To remove any surface bubbles once the resin has been poured, wave the flame of your grill lighter back and forth over the resin. Then, put the mold aside.
4. With a brand-new cup and craft stick, sprinkle some glitter on the cup and then drizzle some resin over it. With the craft stick, stir this mixture just long enough to incorporate the glitter.
5. Put your gem molds with this mixture inside. Work the variety into the corners of the mold using your tweezers or a toothpick (something pointed, of course!). Don't overfill once more.
6. Clear the uncured gems' surface bubbles using your lighter.
7. Until you run out of clear resin or it gets too thick, you can repeat this procedure with different glitters, additives, and mica colorants (whichever comes first).

8. Your resin-filled mold must be set aside to cure. The ideal temperature is just above roor temperature. It won't heal and may even get rubbery if your curing place is too chilly (belov 70 degrees).

9. You can take your jewels out of the mold after the recommended curing time (for me, it wo 24 hours). Not your good sewing scissors! If there is any overfill on the stones, you can carefull remove them and smooth them out with an ordinary nail file.

10. You may now incorporate your finished jewels into various craft projects.

For this two-part epoxy resin, the same additives that you used with the UV resin can be employee including confetti and mica powders. Although it takes 24 hours to cure, the UV resin is slightly mor expensive. Therefore, you might want to try this resin if you have the time and many things to build Ultimately, it comes down to desire and the kind of project you are doing. Both types of resin produc high-quality goods.

What is a Resin Geode?

You can envision what a resin geode may look like if you can visualize a geode. To be precise, geode are geological structures that house colorful mineral stuff inside sedimentary or volcanic rocks. Th rocks' beautiful crystals are exposed when broken or cut open. Of course, a resin geode is not genuine geode.

It's a creative take on a geode made of resin, a substance with a hard, polished texture when it cure To enhance the effects of your resin, you can also add colors, glitter, sparkles, crystals (either real c fake), and metallic paint.

You'll like creating your resin geode if you adore arts and crafts and bright, shiny things. These can b done as relatively flat pieces on a canvas or board, as slices that can serve as coasters, or as mor significant, more sculptural pieces.

How to Make a Resin Geode?

Consider taking a tutorial on using resin if you've never worked with the material before. Even for relative beginners, it's not too harsh, but there are many crucial details to remember. Before beginning, it's critical to understand how to handle resin because certain varieties are hazardous, and all call for protective equipment like gloves and a respirator.

Step 1: Compile Your Materials and Prepare Your Work Area

You'll need the following materials to create geode art with resin on canvas or board:

- Parts A and B of the resin
- Safety equipment: an apron, drop cloths, and latex gloves (a respirator and safety glasses are highly recommended)
- Stirrers and a spatula
- cup or jug for measuring
- tape masking
- Use isopropyl alcohol with wet wipes
- Canvas or wooden panel (not a stretched canvas)
- acrylic colors
- Crystals, foils, glitter, glass globules, and as are examples of decorative objects.

Before blending the resin, prepare everything (always according to the instructions on the label). Put on an apron to protect your clothing, long sleeves, gloves, a respirator, safety glasses, and gloves to protect your skin. Cover your table and flooring with safety drop cloths.

Tape up your canvas's four edges to make it easier to mop resin spills.

Lastly, check to see that your work surface is ideally level (use a level marker, if you have one, to prevent this). In case your surface is uneven, the wet resin will dry unevenly.

Step 2: Draft your Geode Shape

Look through geode pictures to choose the one you want to copy. On your canvas, sketch out the contour and primary forms of the design while keeping track of the colors that should be placed near one another for the most significant outcome. Of course, if you'd prefer to use your resin and ornaments more haphazardly, it's OK.

Step 3: Paint on the Canvas

Fill in any lines or areas you sketched out earlier with acrylic paint by painting straight onto the canvas. This is the moment to embellish your geode pattern using metallic foil or glitter.

Step 4: Incorporate crystals or other embellishments

Once the paint has set, you can add crystals made of glass or acrylic to your design. To prevent them from moving when the resin is added later, secure them with a small amount of regular craft glue.

Step 5: Add Resin Layers

Mix the two components as directed on the resin bottles. To reduce waste, mixing in smaller batches is a brilliant idea. You might now choose to resin by mixing in some paint or powder. You must mix up several resin containers individually and pour them over your canvas surface in stages if you want to have different colored resins next to each other that don't combine. It's up to you if you enjoy the effect of blending various colored resins because some people do. To move the resin where you want it, use wooden sticks.

Step 6: Add Glitter Layers

It's preferable to apply any layers of glitter-embedded resin to your canvas at the very end when the sparkles are closer to the surface. Repeat preparing a small batch of clear resin, stirring in some glitter.

Step 7: Optionally apply a clear coat

You might want to add a final transparent layer on top of your colored and glittery layers because clear resin creates a shiny and flawless finish. The resin geode can resemble an agate piece that has been polished if you do this. The texture of your resin geode may be diminished, though, if you've added a lot of glitter or gemstones. So it's entirely up to you if you apply a final clear coat.

20 Best Crystals & Gemstones For Resin Art

These suggestions for adding crystals and gemstones to epoxy resin are the best. You're in luck if you love to create geode resin artwork or river tables but need some inspiration on what to use for crystals or gemstones. Here, you'll find the BEST geode resin art inspiration with gemstones and crystals! We are completely enamored with the geode art and epoxy resin crafts sweeping the DIY community.

Epoxy resin, glitter, crystals, gemstones, and anything else to mimic the appearance of agate or geode, such as gold leaf or pens for producing lines detailing separating the various hues, are all used to make resin art.

What Gemstone Embellishments Could You Apply to Epoxy Resin Art?

When creating resin art, you can use various materials for your gemstones and crystals. For geode resin art, rose quartz, amethyst, and crystals are frequently used as gemstones in epoxy resin. There are a wide variety of materials available. Choose the finest solution for you with the aid of expert gemstone photography.

Read on to find our beautiful suggestions for making the gemstone or crystal component of your resin crafts, epoxy projects, and jewelry. These resin components are necessary to get dazzling embeds that appear as floating or genuine geodes.

To avoid getting hurt, you must wear the appropriate safety gear before performing any of these techniques. Using the proper respirator, eye protection, and gloves is essential when dealing with resin.

Crystals & Gemstones For Resin Art

Resin for Bulk Gemstones

You can use a wide variety of gemstones in your geode resin artwork. The materials you require for resin crafts, geode resin art, and other projects can be purchased bulk from gemstones. Any creative project benefits from the luxurious touch that raw gemstones bring, and they can be used to make one-of-a-kind, breathtaking pieces of art.

Rose Quartz

Rose quartz is a stunning, functional stone that may be utilized in many resin arts and crafts projects. Its delicate pink color makes it ideal for use in geode resin artwork, and its rough gemstone form works well with more realistic designs. Rose quartz is perfect for anyone wishing to add a touch of refinement to their resin creations.

Bulk Amethyst

Bulk purchases of gemstones like amethyst are frequently far more affordable than individual purchases. This implies that you can use high-quality materials for your resin projects while saving money.

Amethyst is one of the most widely used stones for this purpose. When cast in resin, the gorgeous violet color of raw amethyst looks spectacular. It makes sense why this stone appeals to so many artisans. Adding natural amethyst to your next resin pro will give it that wow factor whether you're a novice or an expert.

Crystal Quartz

Bulk crystal quartz is the best option for artists who wish to give their resin crafts a touch of luxury. This refined form of quartz, often known as rock crystal, has a beautiful sheen that resembles diamonds.

It gives the appearance of a natural geode when used in geode resin art, with its sparkling crystals snuggled inside a smooth outer shell. Quartz and other uncut raw gemstones are becoming more and more common in resin crafts since they enhance the beauty and worth of handcrafted objects.

Crude Amber for Resin

Raw gemstones can provide a dramatic touch to resin jewelry and geode resin art, which might appeal to those who enjoy resin crafts. Amber in bulk is a magnificent material that may be used to make beautiful objects.

The translucent nature of amber resin can assist in highlighting the distinctive shape of the uncut gemstones, and the golden hue provides a cozy and cheery element. Additionally, light, weight, raw amber is perfect for resin jewelry. Further, crafters of all skill levels can benefit from utilizing it because it is so simple.

6. Turquoise Crushed & Tumbled

Turquoise that has been crushed and tumbled is ideal for resin crafts. When utilized to make geode art or jewelry, the raw jewels' vivid blue color is breathtaking. It also makes a beautiful present for resin artists because you can use it to create many resin crafts, including jewelry, geode art, river table, and ornaments. Crushed and tumbled turquoise is ideal if you're looking for a one-of-a-kind gift for a friend or a unique accessory for yourself.

7. Stone Box Mixes

In this store, you may find bulk raw stones for resin artwork. Some people favor buying large quantities of natural rocks to smash themselves. Any resin creation can benefit from the stunning and individual touch that rough stone crystals can offer.

8. Gemstone Kits

This store has many fantastic kits for jewelry and epoxy resin crafts that you can use if you need smaller gemstone pieces and want a more polished finish. Just be mindful of the size of the project you'll be working on, and whether this kit contains enough jewels to complete the entire piece you're working on.

9. For Geodes, Crushed Glass

Crushed glass is essential for anyone who enjoys using resin in their projects. Beautiful jewelry, accessories, and more may be made using it that imitate actual jewels. The best aspect is that it reasonably priced and simple to locate in large quantities. You can mix and match the many hues of crushed glass to make your unique designs. When handling it, be careful because the shards might be sharp. Wear safety goggles and gloves.

10. Sea Glass For Embeds in Resin

Sea glass comprises pieces of weathered glass polished by the ocean's lapping waves (doesn't that sound so soothing?). So it's fantastic if you live close to a beach! You can look for sea glass, gather it, and possibly begin a geode resin sea glass project. Sea glass typically comes in pale blue and green tones.

11. Shells for Resin Art in Geodes

Thinking about geodes with white wave crests scattered throughout and turquoise waves as inspiration while we're on the subject of beaches? So romantic, no? Wouldn't real seashells look stunning in place of gemstones in your geode resin artwork?

We are referring to the interior, which is reflective and iridescent, like a section of an oyster shell or mussel. Here are some dreamy shots for crafts that you can buy for a fantastic price if you want to imitate the beach in your geode resin art for some peaceful and tranquil emotions.

12. Mirror tiles

Your geode resin art will have you oohing and ahhing after you add those reflective bits since they add dazzle and sparkle.

13. Shiny Flat Marbles

These are the ideal way to provide an exposed, "gemstone"-like vibe. You recognize them because you frequently encounter them in fish tanks and flower vases bottoms.

They come in a wide range of colors, and again, depending on the effect you're looking for, you can crush them into tiny bits or keep them whole or partially whole. Every resin artist has to have this on hand!

14. Round Marbles

These bring back memories. As children, we would play with other kids from the neighborhood to see which marbles I could grab while collecting these. But there was always a select handful I refrained from playing with out of concern for failure. Can you identify it?

Because they are all different and unique, those vintage marbles are a fantastic find for your geode resin pours. You can get marbles in solid blocks of color or the original marbles of clear blown glass with colored swirls inside. If you cannot locate your old marble collection, don't worry. I wouldn't want to ruin my early memories and go crazy! (hehe) Grab some instead at a discount.

15. Crystal embellishments in jewelry

If you can find a jewelry-making kit like the one below, you will have many materials. Your imagination is the only thing that will restrict you, from the tiny metal clasps and rings utilized for some attractive and distinctive elements to the beads and stones used.

16. For Geode Resin Art, Gold Leaf

Perhaps you've previously considered incorporating gold, silver, or rose gold leaf in your geode resin artwork. But bet you didn't imagine it being used in this manner: collect some little stones and pebbles from the road or yard, and lightly coat them with Mod Podge or a glue stick. Then cover them with gold leaf, being sure to get the leaf into every nook and cranny of the rocks with a stiff-bristle paintbrush. Now it appears that the pour contains tiny genuine chunks of gold!

17. Decorations for fish tanks

Mainly blue or gold embellishments for resin, fish tank accents provide lovely touches. Fish tank bottoms are frequently coated in a stunning rocky material that would be wonderful for a geode resin art piece. Green, hot pink, blue, and shiny black are all available. You can choose from a wide variety of colors.

18. DIY-Polished Stones & Rocks

Polishing your stones and gemstones is another option. National Geographic is the source of this rock tumbler. Additionally, it starts with half a pound of unpolished, uncut gems. Create your jewels from rocks for geode resin artwork.

19. Swarovski Crystals

Your artwork will become even more collectible thanks to the shine and dazzle added by these stunning crystals. You may achieve the intense glow you're striving for by sprinkling Swarovski crystals here and there.

20.   Fire Glass

We've saved the best for last and are putting an exhilarating, high note on our list of gemstone and crystal suggestions for your geode resin art. Have you heard of fire glass? Imagine one of those stunning contemporary fireplaces with the bottom made of sparkling, brilliant glass. The glass is incredibly reflective and luminous since we located a supplier who doesn't tumble it before delivery.

Furthermore, it is tempered and offered in 10-pound jars, allowing you can use it for large projects. Additionally, you can select either 1/2 or 1/4 size pieces. Alternately, you can use both to create a ring made of more significant reflecting bits and a call made of little geode sections to make it appear more uniform.

Conclusion

s simple to understand why resin is one of the most often used crafting materials. Resin is a flexible, trong, and simple material; it dries transparent, allowing you to make beautiful objects that glitter nd shimmer. You can make gorgeous resin crafts for every occasion with just a little effort. A rock ith colorful crystals inside is called a geode. While some individuals are passionate about finding eodes in the wild, making your resin geode art is a great indoor pastime.

Made in the USA
Las Vegas, NV
30 November 2023